STORY SERMONS
FOR
CHILDREN

With Object Lesson Adaptations

Luther S. Cross

BAKER BOOK HOUSE
Grand Rapids, Michigan

INTRODUCTION

Luther S. Cross, an ordained minister in the United Presbyterian Church, U.S.A., is recognized as one of the leading authorities in the field of religious ventriloquism in this country. For the past twenty years he has been presenting highly successful, original children's sermons. He is the author of the book *Chalk Chuckles*.

In this present book the author's goals are to present children's sermons through the framework of stories, rather than with pious platitudes. He does this through discussing things that children actually do, rather than using adult morals and adult theological terms. Children can see themselves in the stories for they are peopled with children, or with animals and objects that act like children. Heroes and gimmicks that many adult authors *think* would appeal to children — but which only serve to make young listeners lose interest — are avoided. The author appeals to a child's imagination, humor, and sense of wonder. These elements, found in the better secular children's stories, are usually lacking in children's sermons.

The author demonstrates how objects can be used as an integral part of a story presentation, rather than serving to distract from it. He shows how children's chalk talks can be brought up to date with the use of the simple lines of modern cartooning. There is material on the use of puppets to add interest to a children's sermon.

CONTENTS

STORY PROGRAMS

STORY SERMONS

It is more blessed to give than to receive.
—Acts 20:35

1. The Grabby Little Octopus

Once upon a time there was a selfish little octopus whose eight long arms had suction cups on them. All he thought about all day long was using his arms to grab things for himself. He lived in a cold, gloomy part of the ocean. Of course it always seems cold and gloomy around selfish, grabby octopuses or people. When his mother served ice cream for supper, he carefully measured each helping with his eyes to see that he got the most. No matter how much ice cream he got, he would always yell, "Waaaa, you gave sister more than me. You love her more than me."

One day he grabbed his sister's dish of ice cream, and his father's dish, and his mother's dish, as well as his own. "Ha, ha, ha, yick, yick," he laughed. "Now I've got more'n anybody."

His father, mother, and sister were so surprised they just stared at him and looked hurt and hungry. The grabby little octopus felt so guilty that he did not enjoy a single bite of ice cream. It all seemed to stick in his throat.

The next day he and his little octopus friends were playing with their toy dump trucks, when he grabbed every one of the trucks and held them tight in his arms so only he could have them. His friends swam away and would not play with him. He was left all by himself and he felt very lonesome, mean, and unhappy. Nobody liked him. Big salty tears rolled down Grabby's cheeks and made the sea water even saltier. Finally he said, "I don't like myself."

Then he remembered the words of Jesus in his Bible, "It is more blessed to give than to receive."

One Sunday in church school I could hardly believe my eyes. There in the church was a little green octopus...with a big smile on his face, handing out hymnbooks.

7

General Lesson Application

Story sermons 1 and 2 may very well be used together or on successive presentations. The octopus and candle are opposites. The octopus pulls in toward itself to feed; the candle gives of itself to spread light outward. Their environments are opposite. The octopus lives where it is cold, wet, and dark; the candle makes things cheerful around it.

Object Lesson Application

Make an octopus out of a piece of green construction paper, drawing facial features with a black felt point marker or India ink. Cut the teeth out of a piece of white paper and paste on. One side of the octopus has a frown on it while the reverse side is smiling. The smiling side is shown only when it passes out hymnbooks.

Picture or Chalk Talk Application

Most people will prefer to display pictures that are prepared in advance (see p. 92), rather than to make a chalk drawing during a children's sermon. Either method will be effective. We suggest that you at least try your hand at chalk drawing. You may find it easier than you think. If you can master the art of chalk drawing, it will save you much time. And it is very effective. You will not find it difficult to draw the picture as illustrated.

Puppet Talk Application

Use an octopus glove puppet (see pp. 100-101).

Let your light so shine before men, that
they may see your good works and give
glory to your Father who is in heaven.
—Matthew 5:16

2. The Happy Little Candle

A little candle once lived in a gloomy, unused room. He sat around all day, all hunched over, alone, and feeling sorry for himself. It was cold and dark and he had no friends. One day Little Candle read a story about a grabby little octopus that was sad because he always grabbed things with his long arms for himself. It was probably the same story that I told you last week.

"I don't want to be like a grabby little octopus, pulling things in for myself," thought Little Candle. "I am going to give things away to people instead."

Little Candle took a big bag of cookies over to an old lady fly swatter that lived on a shelf in a corner. The elderly swatter was so pleased to have Little Candle visit her that tears of joy shone in her eyes. It was the happiest she had been in years. She thanked him over and over again in her thin, creaky voice. Little Candle felt so glad inside that his face lit up into a smile that shone all around.

Next Little Candle made the beds all by himself to surprise his tired mother. She was so pleased that she sang a happy song all morning. Again Little Candle was so glad that he smiled his bright smile.

Soon everybody that lived in the dark, unused room began to notice that the room had changed into a bright, cheerful room, and that Little Candle was the happiest person there.

General Lesson Application

See p. 8 under this heading for story 1, "The Grabby Little Octopus."

Object Lesson Application

Either display a real candle or make one out of paper, like the illustration. To show the candle's moods better, you could have a sad face drawn on the reverse side.

Picture or Chalk Talk Application

Draw as illustrated, drawing the eyes and mouth last. Draw the smiling mouth at the appropriate time in the story.

Puppet Talk Application

Use a candle glove puppet (see pp. 100-101). In introducing the puppet, show it with the wick and flame piece in its mouth, then remove this and only show it in the puppet's mouth when it is "smiling." If you vibrate the wrist of the hand holding the puppet, it will give the illusion of the flame flickering. The motion is a shortened version of that used in waving farewell, rather than a side to side motion. The gloomy candle may be given a wilted appearance by holding the forearm vertical, but allowing the wrist to hang down limply. If the occasion allows, you may add a little humor at the point when things look brighter for the candle, by saying, "The candle stood up straight." However, the candle remains limp, so you straighten it with the other hand, but it immediately falls again. You very carefully straighten it and it remains thus for a few minutes; but, while you are not looking, it slowly droops over again. This time rebuke it sharply, and it will quickly straighten itself out. Of course the wick and flame piece will not be in the candle's mouth at such times as it is "talking" to you, if you are using ventriloquism.

11

Every athlete exercises self-control in all things. They do it to receive a perishable wreath, but we an imperishable.

—I Corinthians 9:25

3. The Wobble, Wobble, Flops

Junior slammed the piano shut and kicked it.

"I hate practicing the piano," he wailed. "I don't want to be bothered."

Junior's father replied, "You really want to practice, but you don't know it. Because, if you don't practice, you will get a terrible disease, the Wobble, Wobble, Flops."

"Do the Wobble, Wobble, Flops make you get itchy, red spots, or a fever?" Junior sniffed.

Father answered, "Worse than that! They make you so you can't do what you want to do, and you get bored and hate yourself. You get the Wobble, Wobble, Flops through not disciplining yourself; that is, through not practicing every day to learn how to be what you want to be."

The next day, at the roller skating rink, all of Junior's friends had great fun sailing around the floor. All but Junior. It had been too much trouble for him to practice at home on the sidewalk. When he tried to skate, he would wobble, and wobble, and then FLOP, he would hit the floor.

That afternoon, Junior and his friends went out to sail their kites. His friends had patiently made long tails for their kites to keep them balanced, but Junior had not done this as it was too much bother for him. When he tried to sail his kite, it would go up a little ways, and then it would wobble, wobble, and flop to the ground.

That evening Junior wanted to show off in front of everybody at the piano recital. He loved music and wanted to be able to play the piano more than anything else. Alas, he had not practiced. His

12

fingers kept hitting the wrong notes. He wobbled all over the keyboard. Wobble, wobble, flop. Junior was very disgusted with himself.

As they walked home, Father said, "I feel sorry for you, Junior. You have the Wobble, Wobble, Flops. See that sad, dirty, old tramp sitting on the bench there. You are going to grow up to be just like him."

Suddenly Junior realized that he really did want to discipline himself. He really wanted to be able to do things that took practice and work.

"I don't want the Wobble, Wobble, Flops!" he shouted so loud that everyone on the street turned to look at him. So loud that every car on the street stopped and all the drivers looked at him. So loud that all the people in the houses opened their windows and looked at him.

Junior had made up his mind. The next day was Sunday. So he hurried to get dressed to go to church school. He wanted to work hard at learning about Jesus, so he could become a fine Christian.

On his way out, he passed his father sitting in his pajamas, reading the funnies. "How come you don't go to church with us?" Junior asked.

"I went to church school when I was a little boy. Now don't bother me," Father answered.

As Junior walked out the door, he called back to his father, "I feel sorry for you. You have the Wobble, Wobble, Flops."

Object Lesson Application

1. Display a cane, or a pair of crutches, or your arm in a sling, or show a crutch cut out of paper. Label the implement "WWF," to stand for "Wobble, Wobble, Flops." Tell your audience that if you kept your arm in a sling long enough, or similarly abused your leg, it would become weak and unable to serve you with skill. Likewise, when we do not discipline ourselves at something, it makes us weak and handicapped at it.

2. Another approach would be to have Junior's father point out to him that his kite will not fly without the tail (or the string, or both). Similarly, discipline is not a weight or a hindrance but rather a means of blessing. Display either a real kite or a small imitation one made out of a four by six inch filing card cut in the shape of a kite, with a paper tail and a string attached.

13

Picture or Chalk Talk Application

Draw as illustrated, using the first object lesson application given above as the basis for your comments.

Puppet Talk Application

Use a two-faced hand puppet (see p. 97).

1. Tell the story of Junior, with the puppet acting the role of Junior. Use your free hand to represent the piano keyboard and the surface of the skating rink. The puppet would play the piano on top of the back of the free hand and skate on top of its palm. When the puppet falls, bring the palms of your hands (the free hand, and the hand with the puppet on it) together with a clap. Show the puppet as wobbling, by shaking the hand holding the puppet. A miniature kite (see above) could also be used.

2. Another approach would be to present the puppet to the audience with its hand in a sling, or holding a crutch (pinned on). The puppet remonstrates against the discipline of attending church, and instead of telling the story as it is written, you remind him of how he failed at piano playing and kite flying and skating, because he did not practice. The puppet's arm or leg is almost well and he has tried to use it, but found it very weak. Point out to the puppet that when he does not discipline himself at something, it similarly makes him weak and handicapped at it.

Give and it will be given to you.
—Luke 6:38

4. How to Be Happy on Crutches[1]

A little girl named Matilda was making an awful fuss as she walked down Main Street with her father. She should have been ashamed of herself, because it was Christmas time, the season of the birth of our Lord, when everybody should be happy. The streets were ablaze with Christmas lights. The sound of carols was in the air. But Matilda was pouting and crying and pulling back against her father's hand.

Matilda whined, "I don't want a doll house for Christmas. I want a live pony, and a bicycle, and a swimming pool, and a complete wardrobe for my doll because all the other girls are getting them. If you can't give me what I want, I don't want you for my daddy any more. You never give me what I want. I hate you!"

Just then they passed the little crippled newsboy leaning on his crutches. His crutches were decorated with evergreen and holly. He smiled radiantly as Matilda's father bought a paper from him.

"How come you got that holly tied on your crutches?" sniffed Matilda.

The newsboy laughed, 'Everybody seems to have such a sad face, so I decorated my business place, to try to make people smile as they passed."

Matilda was very quiet for the next few blocks. She was ashamed of herself.

Finally her father asked, "Why is it that that crippled boy, who has so little, is so full of joy, and you, who have so much, are acting so miserable?"

In a very small voice Matilda replied, "Maybe it is because he

1 The idea for this story was taken from an article by H. Victor Kane in *The Secret Place*, October-December, 1957.

15

was trying to *give* happiness and I was just thinking about what I wanted to *get*."

Object Lesson Application

Display a paper cutout of a crutch festooned with holly leaves and red berries. On the back side of the crutch there is a red heart with a smile painted on it. The heart represents the love of the crippled boy. Because he tried to make others happy, he himself was happy.

Picture or Chalk Talk Application

Draw as illustrated.

Puppet Talk Application

Use a two-faced hand puppet (see p. 97). Put the puppet on so that the frowning face is on the back side of the hand. This side is used to represent the selfish girl. Hold on to the puppet's hand with your free hand to show her pulling away from her father's hand.

Turn the puppet around so that the smiling side shows, to represent the cripple boy. Place a holly-festooned paper crutch under his arm. A large red heart has already been pinned to his chest, to show that he has a loving nature. His kindness is the reason for his happy smile. If you are using a light bulb hand puppet (see p. 97), flash his smile on after calling attention to his kind heart.

You have no excuse . . . when you judge
another; for in passing judgment upon him
you condemn yourself.—Romans 2:1

5. The Pig in
the Gutter

A big, fat pig named Slander used to wallow in the mud and
filth of a gutter. He was the dirtiest pig in town. He pretented to
be having a good time, but deep down in his heart he was ashamed
of himself. His conscience hurt him so much that he began to make
excuses for himself by pretending that everyone else was as bad
as he, and by saying mean things about them. He was the worst
gossip in town. He accused folks of being show-offs, or of thinking
they were smart, or of being stuck up. Many people were hurt by
his cruel remarks.

One day a gnat flew into the eye of a beautiful girl pig, just as
she was walking by the gutter where Slander was. He thought she
was winking at him and he fell hopelessly in love with her. He
began to take baths and comb his hair and put on after shaving
lotion. He even started to attend church so he could win her favor.
He eventually married the girl pig, and they lived happily ever after.

After Slander's marriage, one of his old, dirty friends phoned
him saying, "Wait till you hear the latest gossip. I heard something
terrible about Mr. Roswell."

Slander smiled a big, fat pig smile, for he had always loved to
hear gossip, but suddenly he stopped smiling. He discovered that
he did not want to gossip any more. Since he was no longer filthy
and no longer ashamed of himself, he no longer wanted to bring
people down to his level.

Slander shouted so loud that the phone was not even necessary,
"No! no! please do not say mean things about Mr. Roswell. I like
him. It would hurt me to hear mean things about him."

Now whenever Slander hears anyone gossip, he feels sorry for them because he knows they are so bad that they feel ashamed of themselves. As a matter of fact, whenever someone tries to gossip to Slander, he gets down on his knees, no matter where he is, and prays, "Dear God, please help that poor pig get clean, so he won't want to say mean things."

I hope Slander never has to say this prayer for any of you.

Object Lesson Application

Display either a toy pig, a piggy bank, a pig cutout from a farm magazine, or a cutout copied from the pictures which accompany this story. Attach a circular piece of white cardboard to the pig's mouth to represent the words coming out of its mouth similar to the "breather" used by a cartoon character. One side of the breather has a skull and crossbones painted on it to represent the evil nature of the pig's gossip. The other side has a heart painted on it to represent kindly words. Similarly the appropriate side of the pig is shown to be dirty, and the other side, clean. A toy pig can be shown to be dirty by taping or gluing pieces of black paper on it. Hold a mirror up to the pig so that it can "see" itself at the right times from either side. Obviously, the dirty pig is the gossip, while the clean pig speaks kindly.

Picture or Chalk Talk Application

Draw as illustrated.

Puppet Talk Application

Use a pig glove puppet (see pp. 100-101). One side of the puppet is "dirty" and the other "clean." Pin a large, irregular piece of black cloth to one side to present dirt. Pin a long, pointed, black tongue to the inside of the mouth. This represents the sharp cutting tongue of the pig. After the pig reforms, fasten a red paper heart to the tip of its tongue to show that it now speaks kindly. A piece of tape folded back on itself to form a sticky circlet will fasten the heart to the tongue. Use a mirror in the same way as you would in the object lesson application.

You shall love your neighbor as yourself.
—Matthew 22:39

6. The Stupid Worm

Once there was a stupid earthworm. He had an I.Q. of zero.

One day the other worms were playing baseball. Stupid Worm had a new necktie, so he walked around the diamond to show it off; but nobody said a word. Finally he stood on his head on the pitcher's mound, but they still did not compliment him on his tie. They just yelled at him to get out of the way.

"That did it!" whined Stupid Worm. "You hurt my feelings. I'm going home and cryyyy. I'm so beautiful and handsome and nobody loves me. I feel sorry for myself."

He crawled down into his hole in the ground and cried for a whole month. He stuck his lower lip out until it looked like a book shelf. This was very stupid because the other worms continued to play baseball and have fun. His crying did not do him a bit of good. He was eight years old and he had only been happy for three and a half days in his whole life. People who let their feelings get hurt usually feel sorry for themselves most of the time. He cried so much his hole got full of water and he started to drown. He telephoned the doctor.

The doctor came, got down on his hands and knees to talk to the stupid worm with the hurt feelings. The doctor was embarrassed. This was the first time he had ever made a house call on a worm.

"What's the matter?" asked the doctor.

"My feelings are hurt and I'm crying," whimpered Stupid Worm. "The other worms were mean to me."

"That is no excuse!" roared the doctor. "This happens to everybody; but sensible people forgive and forget. Jesus was very strong and kind and good. He loved people so much that he couldn't

20

bother with having his feelings hurt. Jesus said that we must love other people as much as ourselves. The only reason you are always getting your feelings hurt is because you think about yourself and nobody else."

The doctor started to leave and Stupid Worm went down in his hole, but then he popped up again.

"Do you know any boys and girls who go to [name of local church] church?" he asked the doctor.

"Of course," replied the doctor.

"Do they ever get their feelings hurt?"

"Of course not!" the doctor yelled. "Do you think they are stupid worms?"

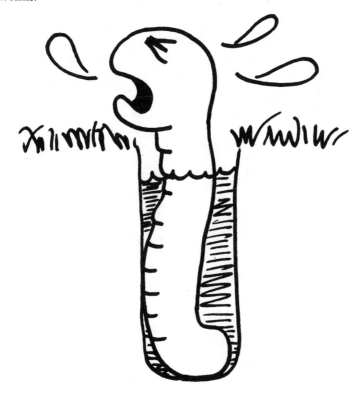

Object Lesson Application

Display a paper cutout of a worm copied from the illustration, or make one by coloring two black eyes on the tip of a light-colored sock. No other features are necessary. The sock will be worn on the hand. Make the worm pop in and out of the ground by holding your free arm out horizontally, and letting it pop up into sight above it, and similarly disappearing from sight. If you are not wearing a pulpit robe, added thickness can be added to your free arm by standing sideways and pulling the lapel of your coat out, so that your coat extends out and below your arm. Simply drop your arm down when you are not calling attention to the fact that the worm is popping in and out. He then is shown in plain sight, although supposedly out of sight. Your free hand will also hold a handkerchief to be applied to the worm's eyes at times during his crying.

Picture or Chalk Talk Application

Draw as illustrated.

Puppet Talk Application

Use a worm glove puppet (see pp. 100-101) according to the directions given above.

As you did it to one of the least of these
my brethren, you did it to me.
—Matthew 25:40

7.   A Gift
to Jesus

"Something is all wrong," exclaimed Lester. "Today is Christmas and Mother and Dad, my brother and I, and the cat and dog have all received more presents than we need, but today is Jesus' birthday and we didn't give him a single thing."

"You're crazy," taunted Big Brother. "How could anybody give Jesus a present? He hasn't been around in two thousand years."

"I'm not crazy," replied Lester. "I just remembered a verse in the Bible that tells how we can give presents to Jesus."

When the family sat down to dinner, Lester heaped his plate full of food and announced, "I'm not going to eat this myself. I'm going to give it to Jesus. I can eat a peanut butter sandwich and the fruit and nuts I got for Christmas instead. I'm going right now and take my dinner to Mr. Sankey next door."

"I thought you hated Mr. Sankey," said Big Brother. "He's a crabby old man. He always phones and complains when you make noise playing outside. He yells at you when you cross his lawn. He's always complaining about you."

"I don't like Mr. Sankey, but I remembered this verse," replied Lester.

Lester knocked on Mr. Sankey's door. It took a long time for him to answer the door as he was old and feeble and had to move about in a wheel chair. His hands shook also. When Lester entered the dark, dingy room where Mr. Sankey stayed most of the time, he noticed that there were no Christmas ornaments anywhere. Later he found that Mr. Sankey had not received a single Christmas present or even a letter. He had just been sitting in his chair feeling blue when he heard the knock at the door.

"Merry Christmas, Mr. Sankey!" blurted Lester. "I brought you a Christmas dinner."

Mr. Sankey looked as though he could not believe someone had brought him a present. Two tears started to trickle down his cheeks. "I didn't know anybody cared about a lonesome old man," he said.

Suddenly Lester knew that he had brought happiness to Mr. Sankey. He really seemed like a nice man when he smiled like that. Perhaps the reason he complained so much was because he was old, alone, and in pain most of the time. Mr. Sankey showed Lester pictures of his wife, who died years ago, and of his past life. He showed Lester every snapshot that he had, and he had many albums full. Lester stayed for three hours while Mr. Sankey told him many exciting stories about his younger days. Lester had a happy glow in his heart. He had found a friend.

When Lester returned home, Big Brother asked, "What was that verse that tells you how to give things to Jesus?"

Lester answered, "In Matthew twenty-five, verse forty, Jesus said, 'As you did it to one of the least of these my brethren, you did it to me.' And I just found out the verse is really true."

Object Lesson Application

Cut out a picture of a man from a mail order catalogue, or make a cutout similar to the picture talk illustration. Cut out a crutch and paste it under the man's arm. Cut out two identical crosses from heavy cardboard. Paste one to the back of your man.

Change the second paragraph of the story to go thus: "You're crazy," taunted Big Brother. "How can you give Jesus a present? Are you going to hang a present on that cross you got in your room?"

At this point display the cross which is not pasted to the back of your man.

As you relate the last sentence of the story, shine a flashlight through your paper so the audience can see the outline of the cross through the man, showing that while you cannot give a gift to Jesus through giving things to a cross in a room, you can give a gift to him through giving to people in need.

Picture or Chalk Talk Application

Prepare your paper by drawing a cross with red chalk, filling the color in solid, on the back side of the sheet. When you begin your talk, quickly draw an identical red cross on the front side of the sheet. The cross will be to one side of where the other cross is located on the back side. Use quick, flat, three-inch strokes, made by applying the length of the chalk against the paper. Next draw the crippled man around the hidden cross as illustrated. The diagonal lines in the illustration indicate the cross you have drawn on the back side of the paper, and which is out of sight. The adaptation and presentation of this story is the same as that done for the object lesson application. When you are ready to shine a light through the drawing, tear it off of the easel, and shine either a lamp or a trouble light, attached to a power outlet, through the paper.

Puppet Talk Application

Use a light bulb hand puppet, featuring a cross that shines through the face (pp. 97-100). Display a paper cross the same size as that which shines through the face. The presentation would be the same as that for the object lesson application.

25

Pride goes before . . . a fall.
                    —Proverbs 16:18

8. The Falls
of Freddie

Little Freddie was in the school principal's office glaring at the principal. The principal was glaring at Freddie.

"Why are you always showing off? Why are you always throwing spitballs, and making funny noises in class, and hitting girls?" the principal demanded.

Freddie said nothing.

"The trouble with you," the principal continued, "is that you have a terrible hunger to be loved. You show off to get attention for yourself. If you could only learn to love other people and be kind to them, you could get over your need for having attention for yourself. In Proverbs, chapter sixteen, verse eighteen, we read, 'Pride goes before a fall.' You will suffer all your life if you don't stop showing off."

One day Freddie's girl friend, Golden Curls invited him to a birthday party. He arrived late on his bicycle so he could make a grand entrance with his wild riding.

"They will know it is the great Freddie when they see me come. Only Freddie can ride a bike like this," he said to himself.

On he came riding like a mad man, with his hands behind his back, instead of on the handlebars. He pretended to be looking the other way, and intended to slam into a sudden halt in front of a group of girls. Alas, he did not see a pile of wet leaves, and down he went in a ridiculous heap, tearing his pants and skinning his knees. The girls roared with laughter. "Pride goes before a fall."

Later on, Freddie insisted on marching into the room with the birthday cake held in one hand over his head, as though he were a waiter carrying in a tray of dishes. Just as he entered the room,

26

someone met him coming through the swinging door. The door hit the cake, knocking it to the floor, where it became a dismal looking gooey white blob. "Pride goes before a fall." All of the children at the party began to hate Freddie.

"See what you did, you big show-off!" they shouted.

Freddie was crushed. He slunk to the back of the room where he noticed someone almost as miserable as himself. It was a shy boy, much younger than the other children. The shy fellow stuttered, and the other children made fun of him. Feeling that nobody wanted anything to do with him, Freddie devoted his time to taking care of the shy boy. He brought him a dish of ice cream and helped him play the games. The little fellow forgot his shyness and laughed in glee as Freddie entertained him. Suddenly Freddie felt good. The shy boy seemed to look up to him. It felt good to be a friend to someone who needed help.

As Freddie rode his bicycle home, he whistled happily.

"It really is true," he thought. "It is a lot more fun being a friend to someone else, rather than trying to show off."

Object Lesson Application

Present a cardboard cutout of a boy, made by either drawing it on cardboard or pasting an illustration from a mail order catalogue on cardboard. The boy's head is made out of an inflated balloon, and is disproportionately large. An expression similar to that shown in the illustration is painted on the balloon with India ink. The easiest way to control the air in the balloon is through using a 1⅜" ball bearing clip, obtained through a stationery store, art supply store, or school art department. Tape the clip to the back of the cardboard boy and use it to hold the head in place and shut off the air. After the last of Freddie's falls, let the air out of the balloon, to show how deflated he has become.

Picture or Chalk Talk Application

Have the deflated balloon, shown in the illustration, already drawn on the page underneath the one on your easel, on which you are to draw before the audience. Draw the inflated balloon-headed boy, as shown, before your audience. At the last of Freddie's falls, tear off the page with the inflated head on it, to show the deflated head.

Make both illustrations, including the bodies, facial features, discharging wind, shadow (underneath the deflated figure) in black outline, with the exception of the outline and shading on the balloons. Make the balloons in red outline. Shading can be added to the inflated balloon

27

by using a flat chalk stroke just inside of one half of the perimeter, as indicated by the shaded area. The heavy circular line on the outside of the shaded area is made of black chalk, and adds further depth to the red shading. The window-shaped box, which represents reflected light, is made in red outline.

Puppet Talk Application

The presentation is the same as that for the object lesson application. An inflated balloon, with features painted on it, represents Freddie's head. This inflated balloon is kept in readiness by having the air secured with a ball bearing clip. Just before your presentation, remove the clip and clip the balloon shut between the index and middle fingers of one hand. The balloon forms the head of a puppet. The body of the puppet should have already been placed on that hand. The thumb and little finger operate the arms of the puppet. The puppet body is a light bulb puppet body (see page 77 too).

9.   The Irreverent Donkey[1]

"Why do you go to church?" brayed the stupid donkey to the wise old owl.

"Because it makes me feel close to God," hooted the owl. "When I walk into God's house, I feel reverent because this is a place of worship. Before the service starts, it seems so quiet and so filled with prayer in church, that God speaks to me. During the hymns, I think about the wonderful words and tunes that God has given us. When we pray with all the people there trusting in God at once, it makes me glad to have a God who hears his children pray. During the offering, I am thrilled to make a gift to God. During the Scripture reading and sermon, I always hear something helpful. I leave feeling inspired for another week."

"What if you go to church and the preacher is no good and you just waste your time?" brayed the donkey.

"Jesus said, 'Seek and you will find,'" replied the wise owl. "If you look for God in church, you will surely find him."

The next Sunday the stupid donkey went to church, but she did not seek God. She found everybody quietly praying before the service, but she began to whisper, "Hee haw, hee haw, hee haw."

The donkey spoiled the reverent quietness for everybody, for the softest whisper can be heard all over a church. If you will listen, you can hear what a whisper way in the back of the church sounds like. [An usher whispers softly in the back of the church.] See how loud a whisper sounds?

The minister began the church service by saying, "The Lord is in his holy temple; let all the earth keep silence before him" (Hab. 2:20).

1 The original idea for this story is taken from the book *Character Sketches,* by George A. Lofton, Southwestern Co., 1898.

Everyone but the stupid donkey felt close to God. She did not hear a word that was said. She spent her time in looking through her purse for bubble gum, thinking about the cute boy who sat next to her in school, looking at a picture of .... [the latest popular teenage singing star] that she found in her purse, counting all of the objects in her purse, picking these things off the floor when she spilled her purse, counting the number of men in church who had bald heads, drawing pictures on her bulletin, and daydreaming that a handsome prince on a white horse was asking her to marry the horse.

When the stupid donkey got home, she sputtered, "That certainly was a waste of time going to church. The minister wasn't any good. It was foolish."

The owl hooted, "The only foolish thing at church today had long ears, and brays."

Object Lesson Application

Display a toy donkey or a paper cutout of one from a farm magazine or copied from our illustration. Also display a piece of cardboard with a rectangular bottom and a roof-shaped top. There is a cross on top of the roof. Call this a "church." The church has a window inside of it, which is merely a rectangular hole cut out of the wall. Make the donkey enter the church by placing the church in front of it. Let the donkey's head be seen sticking out of the window. Remark that, among the other offenses the donkey did, she also gazed out of the window and day-dreamed.

Picture or Chalk Talk Application

Draw as illustrated.

Puppet Talk Application

Use a donkey glove puppet (see pp. 100-101). Cut out a cardboard pew end, such as that shown in the illustration, and hold this up in front of the puppet as though it were sitting in a pew. Make the puppet go through the motions of doing what the irreverent donkey did in church.

If any man would come after me, let him deny himself and take up his cross daily and follow me.—Luke 9:23

10. The Joy of Sacrifice

The missionary from Africa stayed at eight-year-old Faith's house for one night. She and her parents listened to him talk long into the evening. He told them many wonderful things about how he, a doctor, had healed people and taught them to love Jesus. Faith asked him if he liked to watch . . . . . . [name of a popular program] on television, and was surprised to learn that he did not have a television set. He did not have a shiny new car like her folks did. He did not have running water or nice furniture, or any of the comforts that Faith had in her home.

"How could you give up so much to be a missionary?" Faith questioned.

"Why, I haven't given up a thing," laughed the missionary. "The more I do for Christ the more wonderful it is — the more joy and saitsfaction I have in my heart. I wouldn't trade my job with anybody in the world. Besides," the missionary added, "if we would follow Jesus, we must be willing to sacrifice." He said, 'If any man would come after me, let him deny himself and take up his cross daily and follow me.' However, the sacrifices we make for Jesus are really blessings rather than burdens."

The missionary spoke in church the next morning. He told about how much the people in Africa suffered, and how much they needed Jesus. Faith thought about giving the missionary the thirty dollars that she had been saving so long for her new bicycle. Then she thought that it would be silly for her to give up her bicycle when everybody else had one. Perhaps she could give just twenty dollars to the missionary. She thought about this long into the night instead of going to sleep. She remembered what the missionary had said about sacrifice.

For the next eight years, Faith walked to school. She gave up her bicycle for the sake of missions.

The next time the missionary visited her church he brought with him a native boy named David, who had come to America to study in seminary so he could return to preach to his own people.

The missionary told Faith, "David especially wanted to come and see you. It was the thirty dollars you gave that enabled me to perform an operation that saved David's life. His parents were heathens, but at the hospital he and his parents all gave their hearts to Christ."

Faith looked at the fine African boy standing in front of her. Tears came to her eyes. How glad she was that she had given her thirty dollars! She knew beyond all doubt that the sacrifices one makes for Jesus are really blessings rather than burdens. She was the happiest girl in all the world.

General Lesson Application

Story sermons 10 and 26 may well be used together or on successive presentations. The sacrificing girl and the lazy girl are opposites.

Object Lesson Application

Present a cardboard cross and a simple, three-dimensional crown, made out of a strip of golden or yellow paper held together with a paper clip (for easy dismantling and storage). A zigzag row of peaks and valleys along the top of the crown is all that is needed to make it appear to be a crown. A row of red and blue paper circles or squares along the base of the crown could represent jewels. The cross is taped to one end of a one- or two-foot thread, while the crown is taped to the other end. The thread should be of black or transparent nylon, or black silk, to decrease visibility.

Tell how Faith decided to sacrifice, or in effect take up her cross, for Jesus. Hold up the cross just high enough that the attached crown remains on the table. Before this point in the story, have the missionary, after saying that "the sacrifices we make for Jesus are really blessings rather than burdens" add, "When we take up our cross for Jesus, we discover such happiness from it that we know that with God's cross there also comes his reward, or crown of joy. With the cross there comes the crown."

After telling of Faith's joy in meeting the African Christian boy, raise the paper cross higher yet from the table, so that the crown comes into the air with it and is seen to be attached.

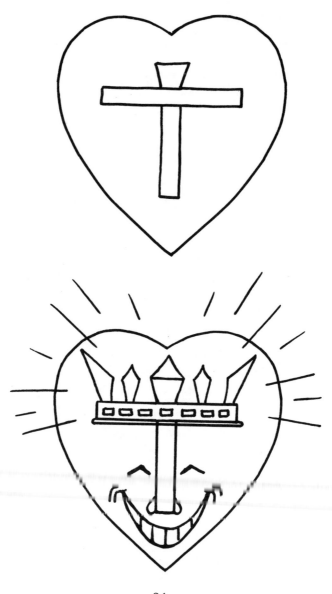

Picture or Chalk Talk Application

Draw the heart with the cross inside it as illustrated, and explaining that the heart stands for Faith's love for Jesus and the cross stands for the sacrifices that people who love Jesus must make. When Faith comes to experience the rewards of her sacrifice, complete the picture as shown in the second drawing; first turning the cross into a crown and then adding the smiling features to show the joy that comes into a person's heart when he sacrifices for Jesus.

Puppet Talk Application

Display a hand puppet. In telling how Faith takes up her cross, fasten a cardboard cross to the back of the puppet. This is done by having a piece of masking tape secured sticky side out to the top of the back of the puppet's costume. It can be held by safety pins, or it can be a circlet of masking tape made with the sticky side out so it will stick to the cloth and to the cross. At the proper time, reach inside the skirt of the puppet's costume from the front and remove the puppet's heart. This is a red paper heart, folded to take up less space. The top of the heart is seen to be crowned with a golden, two-dimensional crown made like the one described in the object lesson application. The bottom part of the heart has a smile painted on it with bold black lines, to be seen from a distance. The explanation of these symbols is the same as that given above in the object lesson application.

Instead of having a smile painted on the heart, it is possible to use a light bulb hand puppet that flashes a smile at the appropriate time (see pp. 97-100).

Even the hairs of your head are all numbered. Fear not, therefore.
—Matthew 10:30, 31

11. Worrying Willie

Worrying Willie was a little boy who always expected something
bad to happen. When the sun shone, he was afraid it would rain.
When it rained, he was afraid that it would forget how to stop.
When he brushed his hair, he was afraid his hair would fall out.
When he brushed his teeth, he was afraid his teeth would fall out.
When he took a bath, he was afraid his skin would shrink and be
too tight for him. When he blew his nose he was afraid it would
stretch out of shape. When he sat down, he was afraid the chair
would break. When he tried to ride a bicycle, he was afraid he would
fall; so he did. When he batted at baseball, he was afraid he would
strike out; so he did. When he took a test at school, he was afraid he
would fail; so he did — because when you think about failing hard
enough, you usually do.

One morning when he woke up he started to worry that it was
going to rain, and it started to rain right in his room. He had worried
so much that a big cloud of gloom had settled on his head. Everywhere he went, he made other people gloomy too, and everywhere
he went it started to rain. His mother had to follow him all day with
a mop. When he ate soup, he had to eat twice as much because it
rained in his bowl. When he went to school, he had to stick his
head out of the window so he would not get the floor wet.

One day, as he was combing his hair, a hair came out on his comb.

"Oh dear! I'm getting *bald*," he cried. "I'll be bald by four o'clock
this afternoon."

He tried to phone the doctor, the police, and the fire department
all at once, to come and save his hair.

Just then he heard a voice saying, "Shame on you. Shame on you for worrying."

"Who said that?" asked Willie.

There was nobody else in the room.

"I did," said the voice.

"Where are you?" said Worrying Willie.

"I'm the hair on your comb."

Willie looked at his comb and saw a hair with a great big number on it.

"How come you have a number?" asked Willie.

The hair replied, "Matthew, chapter ten, verses twenty-nine through thirty-one says that God has numbered all the hairs of your head and that you should not be afraid. Of course this is really just Jesus' way of saying that God loves you very much and watches over you all of the time."

Willie thought about how silly it was for him to worry when God was taking care of him. He smiled a smile that lit up his entire face like the sun coming out, and the cloud of gloom vanished away.

Object Lesson Application

Present a cardboard cutout of a boy, taking the picture from a mail order catalogue or drawing it from our illustration. In the latter case you could draw the reverse side of the boy with a smile such as that shown following Program 21. Make a black paper cloud, with a paper clip taped to the back side of it. In presenting your story, place the cloud on the forehead of the boy, using the clip. At the proper time in the story, lift up a thread from your table. This represents a hair from Willie's head. A long thin piece of paper has been glued to the thread by having the end of the paper glued and lapped over on itself. The paper has a five-digit number printed on it in bold numerals. Willie's new confidence in God can be shown by removing the black cloud and turning the cutout around (if made for this) to show him smiling.

Picture or Chalk Talk Application

Draw as illustrated. Have the paper prepared in advance by having a slit in it at Willie's hairline. In back of the slit there is an envelope pasted onto the back of the paper with rubber cement or plastic glue (which will avoid wrinkling the paper in the manner a water solvent glue would). Inside the envelope is a numbered thread, as described above. A little bit of this thread sticks out of the slit. Thus, after you have completed your drawing of Willie, you can reach up to his head and remove this "hair."

Puppet Talk Application

Use a light bulb hand puppet (see pp. 97-100). Fasten the black cloud to the puppet's forehead and present the numbered hair to the audience in the manner described in the object lesson application.

Several possible light bulb effects are possible. The suggested one is to have a head that has a frown on one side and a smile on the other, but without any colored light effect. With this approach, the frowning side of the puppet would be seen when the palm of the hand was to the audience. At the appropriate time the hand would .be turned around to show the smiling side of the puppet, then after a moment the light would be switched on and the cloud removed from the puppet's brow.

Another possible effect would be achieved by having a light bulb hand puppet with a frown on one side of the head, and a smile on the other, and which makes the head show blue when lighted. With this puppet, the frown would be shown first (worn on the palm side of the hand), and the blue light would be flicked on at times, momentarily, to show spells of increased gloom. At the time for the smile and the removal of the cloud, the puppet would be turned around, but of course the light would not be shown at this point.

12.   The Garbage Can Head

There was a nice little boy named Buddy, but he had nothing to do. So he watched bad programs on television, read bad magazines, and played with a gang of bad boys.

One day at supper his mother asked him to eat his soup and he yelled, "I won't do it, you old witch!"

His father was so surprised that he dropped his false teeth in the soup. The whole family just stared at him. This was not like Buddy at all. Buddy began to cry. He was so ashamed of himself.

Later that day Buddy snatched his baby sister's popsicle and threw it in the mud. Buddy really loved his little sister very much. He could not understand why he was being so naughty.

Buddy asked everybody why he did such awful things. He asked the breadman, the milkman, and the garbageman, but they could not tell him. One day Buddy's hat spoke to him.

"The reason you do such bad things is because you watch and read and listen to bad television shows, books, and friends," said Buddy's hat. "The badness goes into you through your eyes and ears and it comes back out of you through your mouth and hands. The Bible reads, 'Whatever is pure, whatever is lovely...think about these things.'"

"A few bad television programs and books and friends won't hurt me," snorted Buddy.

"Just take me off your head," cried the hat, "and you'll find out what these bad things are doing to you!"

Buddy removed his hat, and felt his head. It felt very strange. It felt cold and hard and round. He ran to a mirror. *His head was turning into a garbage can!*

(To be continued next week.)

Applications for Stories 12 and 13 are combined.

General Lesson Application

Story programs twelve and thirteen are actually one continued story, showing how our minds can either become garbage cans or temples of God. The two stories are designed to be used on successive presentations. It is also possible to combine them into a single presentation.

Object Lesson Application

Display either a metal funnel or one made by rolling up a piece of paper, with one opening larger, and taping it together. Ask your audience to tell you the purpose of a funnel. Tell them that the things that we say, see, hear, and do, with our mouths, eyes, ears, and hands, are things that are funneled into our brain by these organs. Our brains can either become garbage cans or temples of God, depending upon the kind of things we put into them.

In the telling of story twelve, hold up a miniature garbage can to your head, to demonstrate that your mind could become such a thing. You can make the garbage can by either removing the lid and paper label from a tin can, or by making a piece of silver paper into a cylinder. If you hold the cylinder so that your hand covers one opening, it will not be necessary to make a bottom for this type of garbage can.

In the telling of story thirteen, hold up a miniature church to your head. This can either be a cardboard coin box, or any box, such as a match box, with a cardboard roof on it and a cross on the roof, or merely a two-dimensional cutout of a church. Our illustration of Buddy's head could be used as a pattern, by adding a big arched door at the bottom of the temple-head, in place of the facial features, and by omitting the boy's body beneath.

Picture or Chalk Talk Application

1. Draw each picture as illustrated by drawing A.

2. Drawing B shows another possibility. This approach is one that combines the two stories into a single lesson. First show your audience a funnel. Use the lesson application given in the object lesson application above. Alternately fasten a garbage can and a temple of God onto the brain of the boy in your drawing. Cylinders (or circlets) of Scotch tape, made sticky side out, which have been fastened in advance to the garbage can and the temple, will hold them in place. The garbage can is a simple rectangle of silver or light blue paper. It can be copied from our illustration. The temple can be copied from our illustration in the manner indicated in the object lesson application above.

The circular enclosure near the top of the boy's head in this illustration should be described as being his brain. The lines leading to this brain, from his eye, mouth, and ear, should be described as funnels. The funnels and the brain should be of a different color of chalk from that used for the rest of the picture.

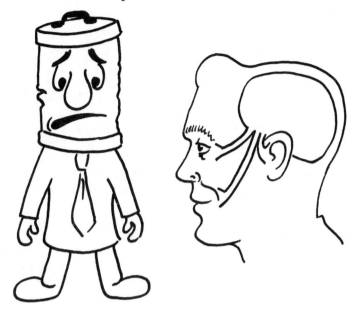

Puppet Talk Application

Use a light bulb hand puppet or a two-faced hand puppet (see pp. 97-100). Use the application given in the object lesson application above. Have the paper garbage can or the temple fastened to the puppet's head in advance. The head of course is a cylinder of paper, and it is prepared by having a paper clip stuck on the top at the front. The garbage can and the temple are not three dimensional, but are two dimensional, and are made as described in the chalk talk application number two, above. It is important that three-dimensional cans and temples not be attempted as they involve more work than one might anticipate, and they are awkward to handle. These two-dimensional symbols are not in harmony with the rounded head of the puppet, but this will not detract from their effectiveness. In the presentations of both stories, the garbage can and the temple are seen affixed over the forehead of Buddy, and in both instances they are initially covered by a hat that is removed at the appropriate time in the story. The hat is also two dimensional and is held in place over the can or temple by the same paper clip that holds them. A sample hat, to be copied, is found on page 25.

41

I can do all things in him who strengthens
me.—Philippians 4:13

13. The Temple of God

Last week we told you about a boy named Buddy, who read so
many bad books and put so many bad things into his head that it
turned into a garbage can.

Can you imagine how embarrassing this was?

How would you like to have your friends yell, "Ha, ha, ha,
Garbage Head."

How would you like to have little children take the lid off your
head and put bubble gum wrappers and banana peels into it?

When Buddy went to church school, he would always climb in a
back window and sit behind the piano, so people would not see his
head. One Sunday the teacher told the class about how the Apostle
Paul said that he could do all things through Christ who strength-
ened him.

Buddy thought to himself, "Only Christ can give me the strength
to bear my disgrace; so I had better learn all about him."

Buddy began to read his Bible every day. He also read about the
lives of missionaries and other men who loved Christ. He was so busy
reading about Christ, that he did not have time to read his bad
magazines.

One day Buddy was sneaking into church school, when some of
the people happened to be standing in the back of the church where
they could see him. Just then a gust of wind came by and blew off
his hat. He hung his head. He did not dare look up and see how
horrified the people would be when they saw his garbage can head.
Finally he looked up out of the corner of one eye and saw that they
were smiling at him. They were talking about what a fine boy he
was and what a beautiful face he had. You see, he had read so much

about Christ that his mind had turned into a temple of God instead of a garbage can. It did not really look like a temple of God on the outside, of course, but the love of God shone in his face.

Lesson Applications

See application following Story 12.

Love is patient . . . not irritable.
—I Corinthians 13:4, 5

14. Angry Anthony

There was a boy named Angry Anthony, who was always losing his temper. He must have been very selfish, because only very selfish people are always doing this.

One day his mother called him to dinner while he was watching cartoons on television. When he refused to come, she took him by the hand. His face got redder and redder and redder. He lost his temper. He yelled so loud that all the cars stopped at the train crossing. They thought that they heard the train whistle. He kicked the television set into splinters and got a nasty headache that lasted for a whole day.

The next day Angry Anthony was learning to ride his bicycle when he fell off. His face got redder and redder and he lost his temper. He yelled so loud that all the factory workers went home to lunch. They thought they had heard the noon whistle. He took a hack saw and cut his bicycle into little pieces and got a nasty headache that lasted a whole week.

Later on Angry Anthony was playing baseball when he struck out. His face got redder and redder and redder. All the other children ran for cover. The birds in the trees hid their heads under their wings. He lost his temper. He yelled so loud that all the volunteer firemen came dashing into town. They thought the fire siren had sounded. He broke all the bats and threw the ball into a trash fire, so nobody could play ball. He got a headache that lasted a whole month.

After that he had to live in the doghouse, because nobody would have anything to do with him.

"Nobody in the whole world likes me but you," he told his dog.

"That's not true," said the dog. "I don't like you either. You yell so loud you hurt my ears."

"What can I do to make people like me?" asked Angry Anthony.

"Well, I don't want to sound personal," said the dog, "but why don't you stop losing your temper? The thirteenth chapter of First Corinthians reads, 'Love is patient . . . not irritable.' A follower of Christ should never lose his temper the way you do."

"How can I control my temper? I've got the worst temper in the state of _____ [name of state you live in]."

"Anybody can learn to control his temper," replied the dog.

"Anybody?"

"Certainly, anybody. Lots of people have terrible tempers, but they learn to control them."

So Angry Anthony took his head off, unscrewed his temper and threw it into a wastebasket, and he has never missed it since.

Object Lesson Application

Tape a flesh-colored or white square of paper to a small cooking pot. The paper will have a smiling face drawn on it. Tape a piece of red construction paper on the opposite side of the pot. The red paper will have a frowning face on it. See following Story 21 for sample faces. Show the smiling face to the audience as you present the pot to it, to represent Angry Anthony. Whenever Anthony loses his temper, turn the pot around to show the red face. As a climax to his losing his temper, let him blow his lid (lift up the lid from the pot).

When Anthony decides to get rid of his temper, lift the lid and remove a piece of cardboard labeled, "TEMPER," and put this into a wastebasket.

Picture or Chalk Talk Application

Draw as illustrated.

Puppet Talk Application

Use the red-faced light bulb hand puppet described on pages 97-100. The frowning face is shown exclusively until the time Anthony discards his temper. His loss of temper is shown by switching the bulb on so that his face becomes red. When Anthony discards his temper, remove the paper head cylinder, unscrew the light bulb and put it into a wastebasket. Replace the head cylinder, clipping it in place between the middle and index fingers of the hand wearing the puppet and *then* turn that hand around so that the back side is visible to the audience and they can see the smiling face.

If anyone strikes you on the right cheek,
turn to him the other also.—Matthew 5:39

15. The Other Cheek and Spider

Corky was a lonesome boy. There were no other small boys on his block except Spider and he did not like Spider at all. Spider was the best fighter in the third grade.

One day Corky was building himself a club house out of old boards. It was a lot of work just to take the nails out of the boards so he could use them. Then along came Spider.

"Well, what have we here?" said Spider. "I'm a building inspector. I have to kick new buildings to see if they pass inspection."

With that, Spider kicked Corky's house down and helped himself to the best boards.

"Give me back my boards," whimpered Corky. He was furious. He thought to himself, "I would like to get a club and beat Spider's face till it was all bloody! I would like to get a gun and shoot him!"

Corky was so angry that everything went wrong for him. He hit his thumb with his hammer three times and cut himself with his saw. He spilled his soup at supper and yelled at his mother and was sent to his room with nothing to eat. When he tried to do his homework, he made so many mistakes that the teacher gave him a poor grade the next day.

That night at family prayers, Grandpa read these words of Jesus from the Sermon on the Mount: "If anyone strikes you on the right cheek, turn to him the other also. . . . Love your enemies and pray for those who persecute you."

"Everything has gone wrong with you because you are angry," said Grandpa. "You heart is weighted down with a load of hate. Try returning Spider's meanness with love and that load of hate will go."

"Being good to Spider would just make me feel worse!" snorted Corky.

"You try it," said Grandpa, "and if it works, promise me you'll come and tell me about it."

"I won't have to tell you anything, cause it won't work," yelled Corky.

The next day Corky was working on his club house, when he heard Spider's taunting voice.

"Here is your favorite building inspector. Have you got some more boards for me today?"

Corky replied, "Help yourself, and here's a whole stack of even better boards. Take all you want."

Spider's mouth dropped open in surprise. "What's the matter with them? Don't you want them?"

"Oh, I got lots of them. Here's an old hammer we don't need and some nails. Why don't you make a club house too?" said Corky.

Spider looked confused. "Aw, who wants to build an old club house? Why don't I help you. A building inspector could help real good. You tell me what do do."

They worked together all afternoon.

Finally Spider said, "Say, I know where we can get three other guys to join our club and we can hold meetings."

"Yeah!" squealed Corky. "You can be the president and I'll be the vice-president, and we can go on safaris and kill elephants and have a secret language 'n' everything! Come back tomorrow and we can finish the house. I gotta quit now. I gotta tell Grandpa something."

Object Lesson Application

Display a cardboard cutout of a boy as described in the Object Lesson Application following Program 11. Make paper cutouts of a heart and a bottle of poison as shown in the illustration following this program. Tape the poison bottle to the chest on the unhappy side of the boy and tape the heart to the chest on the happy side. Explain that Corky is unhappy because he has a load of hate in his chest. When Corky is kind to Spider, turn the boy around and explain that Corky is happy because he has love in his chest. The heart stands for love and the poison bottle stands for hate.

Picture or Chalk Talk Application

The heart and poison bottle shown in the illustration are not a part of the chalk drawing. They are paper cutouts that have Scotch tape

circlets (made with the sticky side out) on their backs. Use the same presentation as that made in the object lesson presentation. The smiling face is drawn before you meet your audience. It is hidden from sight by the poison bottle of hate. Draw the rest of the boy including the frowning face in front of your congregation. Explain that Corky's hate makes him unhappy. At the proper time in the story cover the frowning face with the heart cutout that represents love, then remove the poison bottle, to show that Corky is now happy.

Puppet Talk Application

Use either a two-faced puppet or a light bulb puppet (see pp. 97-100). Have the poison bottle taped to the chest on the sad side and the heart taped to the chest on the puppet skirt on the happy side of the puppet. The presentation is the same as that for the object lesson application. In case you use a light bulb puppet, where the sad face changes to the happy face through light on the same side of the head, have the heart taped underneath the poison bottle on the chest and remove the bottle at the appropriate time to reveal the heart.

Watch and pray that you may not enter
into temptation; the spirit ... is willing,
but the flesh is weak.—Matthew 26:41

16. Andrew's Picture

A weak, dirty, ugly bum named Andrew was sitting in the gutter, half asleep, when he found a beautiful picture of Christ. Tears came to his eyes as he looked at the strong, clean, good face of the Savior. Jesus was so good and Andrew was so bad. He longed with all of his heart to become more like Christ. He began to talk to his picture each day and it seemed as though the picture answered him.

One day Andrew saw a drunken man lying on the sidewalk. He started to roll him over and steal his pocketbook, but just then he heard the voice of Christ saying, "You can't do that because I am with you."

"Oh, yes, I can! I've always done it," snorted Andrew.

But he found that he could not do it. The wonderful, clear, true eyes of Christ seemed to be on him and he did not want to do anything so evil.

As Andrew talked to his picture of Christ every day over the years, he even began to look like the picture. He began to act more and more like Christ. He even got himself a job, painting pictures for a company that sold waterproof books to schools of fish. He had a beautiful office with red wall-to-wall carpet.

Andrew became so busy with his job that he forgot about his picture of Christ. Without his picture to guide him, he drifted back to his old bad self. He became a weak, dirty bum.

One day he was so drunk that he spilled his jar of ink, making a big black spot on the beautiful rug in his office. He tried to clean it but he fell asleep right in the middle of it. Just then his boss came in and fired him on the spot.

In desperation Andrew found his picture and began to talk to it every day again.

"I'll never, never, never try to live without my picture again," he cried. "It is the only thing that can keep me straight."

In later years Andrew became such a fine man that people came from miles around to ask him the secret of his life.

"The whole secret of my life has been my wonderful picture of Christ," he would always tell them.

One day a great crowd of people asked Andrew if they could live good lives if they also had pictures of Christ.

"Of course you can," replied Andrew.

"Where can we get pictures of Christ like yours? What company prints them?" the people asked.

Andrew replied slowly, "This kind of a picture is not the kind that can be printed on paper. It exists only in my heart. I have always called it talking to Christ. Another name for it would be daily prayer."

Object Lesson Application

In telling the story of Andrew, pretend to be holding a picture in front of your eyes, using both hands. When Andrew reveals that his picture really exists only in his heart, remove a large paper heart from

the vicinity of your heart. It could be in a vest or shirt pocket. On the heart there is a picture of Jesus. It is either a printed one that has been cut out or one drawn with simple lines, such as that shown in the picture illustration.

Picture or Chalk Talk Application

Either draw the picture of a bum as illustrated and tear it off at the proper time to show the picture of the reformed Andrew (which has been drawn in advance) on the sheet of paper beneath, or draw both of them, side by side, in front of your congregation. The heart is a paper cutout made in advance from red paper. A sticky-side-out circlet of Scotch tape is on the back of the heart, so that it can be stuck on the chest of the reformed Andrew at the appropriate time. The heart has either a silhouette drawn on it or a printed picture of Christ, cut out in silhouette, and pasted on it.

Puppet Talk Application

Use the same presentation as that of the object lesson application. Use a light bulb hand puppet or a two-faced hand puppet (see pp. 97-100). One side of the puppet's head could have a face with unkempt cotton hair and a dark shadow on the lower face to indicate the need of a shave. This side would show the unhappy face of a bum. The other side of the head could show a happy face. Also a head showing happy and unhappy faces could be used, without making one face specifically that of a tramp. When Andrew reveals the secret of his picture, remove a heart with a picture of Jesus (made as described in the chalk talk application) on it, from under the puppet's skirt.

What is a man profited, if he shall gain
the whole world, and lose his own soul?
(K.J.V.)—Matthew 16:26

17.   The Greatest,
Animals There Are[1]

"I'm going to invent a new animal," said little George as he
scribbled with his pencil. "It's going to have the biggest of everything — the biggest neck like a giraffe's to look in upstairs windows,
the biggest nose like an elephant's to sneeze with, the biggest ears
like a rabbit's to hear with, the biggest tail like a squirrel's to wave
with. It'll have an alligator's mouth, a pig's tummy, and a cow's udder, so it can bite the biggest, eat the most, and give the most milk.
When people see my animal they will say 'Hooray! hooray! for
George. He has made the animal with the biggest parts that ever
was.'"

Grandpa laughed, "Why I am looking at an animal right now
that has something far bigger and more important than anything
your animal has."

"Where Grandpa? I don't see any animals in this room."

"I'm looking at you," said Grandpa. "People are a kind of animal
too."

George looked at himself in the mirror over the mantel. He looked
at his small nose, ears, neck, body, arms, and legs. He seemed very
tiny compared with some of the animals that he had seen at the zoo
that morning.

"You're kidding," he replied.

"No, indeed," said Grandpa. "You have something big that no
other animal has. God made people with big souls."

"What's a soul, Grandpa?"

1 Adapted from a children's sermon, "You Have a Big Soul," by Arthur W. Mielke,
Copyright 1954 by the Christian Century Foundation. Reprinted by permission from *The
Pulpit*, March, 1954.

"A soul is something that makes us able to love and worship God and love and help other people," replied Grandpa.

"How about that, Gramp?" squealed George. "We are the greatest animals there are."

Object Lesson Application

Show toy animals or pictures representing several of the creatures mentioned in the story. In addition show a paper heart representing the human soul.

Picture or Chalk Talk Application

Draw as illustrated.

Puppet Talk Application

Use a glove puppet animal having the features of the animal shown in the picture talk application (see pp. 100 101). The cow's udder could be omitted, while the alligator's mouth and pig's tummy could be indicated merely by oral identification, rather than through alterations in the puppet's body.

Blessed are the poor in spirit, for theirs
is the kingdom of heaven.—Matthew 5:13

18. The Oyster's Advice

A girl named Nancy was so ugly that when she was down on her hands and knees, people thought she was a bulldog. She always wore her hat backwards so it would hide her face. She kept very busy doing nothing. Sometimes she was too busy to eat her meals. Sometimes she was too busy to sleep.

When her mother asked her what she was so busy doing, she would say, "Feeling sorry for my ugly face."

One day she was feeling sorry for herself in an aquarium, which is like a zoo for fish.

She was walking past an oyster, asleep in his shell, when she said, "I am the most unlucky girl in the world."

The oyster said, "No, you're very lucky! You can make your trouble into a thing of beauty, like I do. I have terrible sharp pieces of sand in my shell that hurt my soft body, but I cover the sharp sand with smooth layers of pearl that I secrete with my body. Then the sand no longer hurts me and I have made a pearl of great beauty."

Nancy remembered what the oyster had told her about making her trouble into something beautiful. Perhaps she was fortunate after all. She spent the rest of her life being a friend to everyone, being cheerful, kind, and helpful. She never gave her ugly face a thought again. Everybody loved her. And you know something? They all called her the lady with the kind face.

Object Lesson Application

Display either a small sharp rock, or a wadded up piece of black paper, and a Ping-Pong ball. These are identified as the irritating piece of sand and the pearl of great beauty that it is transformed into.

Picture or Chalk Talk Application

Draw as illustrated, drawing the irritation in the girl's heart next to last and adding the circular pearl around it last. The two holes in the hat are eye holes so that Nancy can see where she is going.

Puppet Talk Application

Use an oyster glove puppet (see pp. 100-101). Have the piece of sand and the pearl (rock and Ping-Pong ball), as described in the object lesson application, inside of the oyster's shell. Remove them with your free hand as the oyster describes his problem to Nancy.

Do all things without grumbling.
—Philippians 2:14

19. Complaining Connie

Complaining Connie was a girl who reminded everyone of a skunk. She made her stink with her mouth instead of her tail. She was always saying four words that made everyone unhappy.

One morning, Mother fixed scrambled eggs and tomato juice for breakfast with loving care. She was happy because she had worked hard to please her family.

"How do you like your breakfast, dear?" Mother asked Connie.

Then Connie said her four terrible words that made Mother, Father, and Brother sad. The sunshine was gone from the kitchen. Only gloom remained.

"I don't like it," pouted Complaining Connie.

Those were her four terrible words.

At church school that day, all the boys and girls were dressed in their very best suits and dresses. They all seemed to be very glad that it was Sunday morning and that they were in God's house. The teacher smiled a bright smile and asked the children if they would like to hear a story about Jesus healing a blind man.

Complaining Connie said, "I don't like it."

All the nice smiles vanished.

No matter what hymn the teacher wanted the class to sing, or what activity she wanted them to do, Connie would always say, "I don't like it."

That night the rest of Connie's family decided that they would all complain too, so Connie could see what she sounded like.

At supper that night, Mother tasted her salad and said, "I don't like it."

Father tasted the soup and threw his spoon down.

"I don't like it," he sputtered.

57

Brother tasted his milk.

"I don't like it," he growled.

"I don't like it. I don't like it. I don't like," said everyone.

Complaining Connie knew they were imitating her. She felt *this* big. (Hold your thumb and index finger about an inch apart.) She got out of her chair and went to the mirror to see if she really were *this* big. (Demonstrate again.)

"Why am I the only one that usually complains?" she asked the mirror.

The mirror replied, "The real reason you complain is because you are selfish and want your own way — your favorite breakfast, your favorite stories, hymns, and activities in church school."

Connie never complained again, and when she hears someone else complain she always says, "Oh dear, that poor person is turning into a skunk."

Object Lesson Application

1. Make a paper cloud out of black construction paper. Make the cloud trail off into a small stream, so that it will look like the one in the chalk talk illustration. Add the following words to the first paragraph in the story: "These four words were like a black cloud of gloom that came out of Connie's mouth."

As you say this turn the side of your face to the congregation and hold your paper cloud so that it looks like a black cloud coming out of your mouth. Repeat this action every time Connie complains.

2. An alternate method would be to paint a frowning face on a balloon (see illustration following Story 8). Inflate the balloon and secure the air in it with a ball bearing clip. At the proper time, remove the clip and hold the neck of the balloon between the thumbs and index fingers of both hands, stretching it, so that a whining sound is made. This represents Connie's complaints and could be repeated at the appropriate times in the story.

Picture or Chalk Talk Application

Draw as illustrated.

Puppet Talk Illustration

Use a two-faced or light bulb hand puppet (see pp. 97-100), changing the faces at the appropriate times in the story. Make and use a black paper cloud in the manner described in the object lesson application, except that the cloud is held to the puppet's mouth.

Let your light so shine before men, that
they may see your good works and give
glory to your Father who is in heaven.
—Matthew 5:16

20.   Who Is Leland?

Leland was a boy who used to think about Jesus very much. He
thought that it would be the most wonderful thing in the world
if only people could know the Savior in person as the disciples did
many years ago. Leland felt sure that everyone would want to be
Christians if they could only see Jesus put his arms around little
children, and heal the sick, lame, and blind, and teach marvelous
things about God.

When a new boy came to school, who stuttered, walked with a
limp, and wore funny looking clothes several sizes too large, most
of the children laughed at him, especially the school bully. However,
Leland did not laugh, but instead sat beside the new boy in class
and was a friend to him. This took real courage because they began
to make fun of Leland also. When the new boy was sick it was
Leland who came to his home every day with books and helped
him with his homework.

Leland was always helping people. There was the time a fat
lady dropped her groceries, and he helped her pick them up and
carried them ten blocks to her home. Again there were some children
who laughed at the lady and at Leland for helping her. The bully
even threw rocks at Leland.

Eight years later the bully became a Christian and joined the
church.

When the minister asked the bully why he had accepted Christ,
he replied, "Because I was able to see Jesus in the way Leland lived,
and I knew that I wanted to live that way too."

This is the only way anybody can see what Jesus is like — to be able to see him in somebody's life.

I think this is a very beautiful story and it is a true one, except it has not happened yet and I do not know what kind of things Leland is going to do, or whether he is a boy or a girl, but I do know that he or she could be sitting right here in this room, and I have his or her picture here. (Hold up a large mirror so that its back is to the congregation.) I do not want to embarrass the person here who could become like Leland, but here is that person's picture. (Turn the mirror around and show from side to side so that each child can see his own reflection mirrored.)

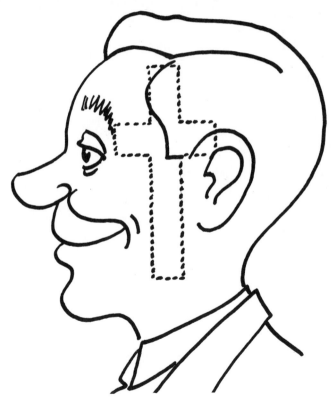

Object Lesson Application

Use a mirror as indicated in the story program.

Picture or Chalk Talk Application

Draw as illustrated. Dotted lines indicate a cross that has been drawn in advance on the back side of the paper. See page 92ff. for details of setting this up and presenting it. The cross is revealed in the face at the appropriate time. After showing the congregation that people saw Christ in Leland, use the mirror as indicated in the story program.

Puppet Talk Application

Use a light bulb hand puppet (see pp. 97-100) which lights up to make a cross show through the facial features, or else use a two-faced hand puppet made with two smiling faces. One face has a red cross drawn underneath the features. This is revealed at the appropriate time. Use a mirror as indicated above.

Object Lesson Application

Display a Bible. Before telling the story, comment that some people read their Bibles very little. For them it is just a book full of old memories, like faded flowers that are pressed in a book. These people will not grow from their Bible reading. Their faith is apt to be sort of pressed and dead like this flower. (Remove either a pressed flower from the Bible, or a paper imitation of one, such as the one in our illustration.) Other people study their Bibles everyday and it helps them to gain a strong, happy faith. (Remove a large heart to demonstrate. This heart may have a smiling face such as shown, and it may have some device attached to it to show strength, such as a pair of muscular arms or a picture of a dynamo or an electric motor.

Other things which might be removed from the Bible, in this or another object talk, are a pocket mirror, a road map, and a cardboard cutout of a bottle of milk, to show that in the Bible we find a mirror of, and a better understanding of our secret faults, guidance in life, and food for spiritual growth.

Picture or Chalk Talk Application

Draw as illustrated, using the method described above.

Puppet Talk Application

Use the presentation and the objects described in the object lesson application, but add a hand puppet cast in the role of Alan. The sermonizer could cast himself in the role of Grandpa and give all of his dialogue in answer to Alan's questions. (See page 98 for ways to make a puppet "talk.")

He who loves his life loses it, and he who hates his life in this world will keep it for eternal life.—John 12:25

23.   The Lost Load

Laddy had been naughty at summer camp. He got away from his counselor and fell over a bank, broke his arm and got his body covered with hives from poison ivy. His face was so swollen that none of his friends recognized him. He itched so much he could hardly stand it. However, his counselor was very patient. He drove Laddy to the doctor's office to get his arm set and waited on him constantly.

"I don't see why you waste so much time helping me," said Laddy to his counselor.

The counselor replied, "I like helping you. We are not really happy ourselves unless we help others; because God made us that way. When you see someone who is gloomy and feeling sorry for himself, you know he is thinking about himself. When we help with someone else's burden, our own load goes away."

Later that day, Laddy sat on the bank of the river and watched the other children swim. He loved to swim more than anything else but, of course, he could not go in. His arm ached like a sore tooth. He itched all over. He listened to the happy shouts of his friends. He had come to camp to have a good time and now it was all ruined. He remembered how his counselor had said, "When we help with someone else's burden, our own load goes away."

"Baloney," thought Laddy, "nothing could make me feel good right now."

Just then Laddy saw Winfield, the little boy who was visiting camp that afternoon with his father. He was hardly more than a toddler. Winfield stumbled over a tree root and the box of popcorn that he had been eating so contentedly spilled all over the ground. Winfield felt about the ground, trying to find his popcorn. Suddenly Laddy realized that Winfield was completely blind.

"Come on," said Laddy, "I'll help you pick up that dirty popcorn and go buy you another box. I have some money in the camp bank."

Laddy took Winfield's hand and led him back to the camp store. He took him all over the camp and explained everything to him. He let him feel the tents and the cots. Laddy had only known Winfield for a couple of hours, but already he felt that he loved the little fellow. In spite of his blindness, he was such a cheerful boy. Winfield laughed at Laddy's jokes, and seemed to appreciate everything Laddy did for him.

When Winfield's father came to take him home, Winfield said, "Daddy, this is my friend, Laddy. He 'splained the whole camp to me. He's the nicest boy in the whole world. When I get home you are going to help me write a letter for him."

Winfield insisted on kissing Laddy goodbye.

Laddy felt ten feet tall. As a matter of fact, just then he did not have a care in the world.

Object Lesson Application

Display a rough-shaped, black, paper oval, which is described as a load. Remark that everyone has some load to bear. Tell about Laddy and his load. Tell how Laddy showed love to Winfield. Fasten a red paper heart over the black paper "load," securing it with a sticky-side-out circlet of masking tape which has been fixed to the back of the heart. The heart represents love and assistance. When the heart is in place and at the proper time in the story, unfold paper wings, which are folded in back of the heart. This represents the fact that when we help someone else, our own load takes wings and flies away. If you make the wings smaller in proportion to the heart shown in the drawing, and make the wings and heart similar to the drawing, the wings will easily fold out of sight behind the heart.

Picture or Chalk Talk Application

Develop this application in the same manner as the object lesson application above. First draw the boy and his heavy load. At the proper time add what is shown here as a dotted line, but which will be drawn as a continuous line. This turns the load into a load with a heart on top of it. At the proper time add the wings and the shadow underneath the boy and change the boy's expression into a smile like that shown on the face to the left of the boy. This is done by extending and enlarging the sorrowful mouth into a smile. The head to the left of the boy is not meant to be drawn beside the boy, but merely shows an alteration to be made in the boy's face.

Puppet Talk Application

Develop this application in the same manner as that indicated for the object lesson application. Use a hand puppet. Hold the puppet in a bent over position so that his back presents a horizontal surface. Place a "heavy" load upon his back. The load can be a wad of dark paper, or a sock stuffed with some other socks to have a ball-like appearance. Apply a paper heart of the kind described above to the load, sticking it there with tape. At the proper time, open the hidden wings and make the load "fly" off of the puppet's back.

24. The Girl Who Saw Good in Others

In a dark woods there was a terrible robber who lived with a horrible wife who nagged and yelled at him with a voice that sounded like a herd of angry elephants trumpeting. The robber's father, who was a drunken bum, lived with them. He did nothing all day but lie around in a drunken stupor and carve sticks of wood.

One night the robber woke up and discovered that someone had entered his house and was asleep on the living room rug. It was a little girl named Joy. She was sleeping with her head on her handbag.

The robber gently lifed her and put her on the sofa so he could steal her handbag. Just then Joy woke up.

"I knew you wouldn't mind if I came into your house to sleep," she smiled. "I was lost in the woods. You remind me of my daddy. You are handsome and kind like he is."

The robber almost fell over in surprise. Nobody had ever told him he was handsome and kind before. He ran to look in the mirror.

As they all sat down to breakfast, the horrible wife was getting ready to curse her husband, when Joy cried out, "What a wonderful cook you are. My! those pancakes smell good."

The horrible wife stood there with her mouth open. If this dear child thought she was wonderful, she should not yell at her husband just now.

After breakfast Joy looked at some of the animals that the drunken father had carved. Her eyes grew wide with admiration.

"You must be the best carver in the whole world," she said.

The old drunk had started to reach for his whiskey, but he

stopped. If the little girl thought he was wonderful, perhaps he should not disappoint her.

Little Joy had to wait several weeks for her father to come and get her, so she lived with the robber and his family. Before she left their lives were completely changed. She thought they were so wonderful, that they began to act like good people rather than disappoint her.

After Joy left the reformed robber, she had many happy adventures. Her heart was so full of love that she could always see good in people and wherever she went she always made people better.

Is this story true? Yes and no. It did not really happen exactly like this, but I do know some people who always see good in others, and they really do make other people better, and it really does seem as though God is very close when they are around.

Object Lesson Application

Display a paper doll, or a girl cutout made from a picture in a mail order catalog. The girl has large red hearts on her face to serve as eyes, showing that she sees through the eyes of love. This girl represents Joy. When the fact develops in the narration, that she brings out good in others, cause a cross to be seen shining through her body. (Body has cardboard cross glued to back. Shine light through it.)

Picture or Chalk Talk Application

Draw a picture of a heart and turn it into the robber, with a frown on his face. The heart shows that there is hidden good in him. Draw the picture of a little girl, to his side, next. Her heart-shaped eye shows that she sees good in him. As a result of this he changes from a frowning evil man to a smiling good man. The bottom, heart-faced man is not an additional picture to be drawn on paper, but is the second stage of the robber. It shows how more moustache is added to cover up his angry mouth, and how a smiling mouth is added beneath it. It also shows how the robber's eyebrows have their lines extended into a half circle, and how pupils are added in those half circles, so that his frowning eyebrows become the bottom lines of smiling eyes. Up-turned eyebrows are also added. The man has his face changed at the appropriate time in the story.

Puppet Talk Application

Use a puppet like the kinds described on page 93. Cause a cutout of girl, like that described in the object lesson application above, to be brought into the puppet's presence. The puppet represents the robber. When the cutout sees good in the robber, he changes and Christ is seen to be in his life. Show the cross shining in or through the robber's face (a light bulb puppet face).

Puppet Talk Application

Use the same presentation as that given in the object lesson application. Show a small doll or cardboard boy as indicated above. At the proper time have him engulfed by a glove puppet (see pp. 100-101). The glove puppet is of course cast as a germ, and is present throughout the story. He comments through one of several devices (see page 101) about his ability to grow and surprise the boy, and about his evil nature. Make a miniature, two-dimensional paper replica of the glove puppet germ, which the boy is to handle (become taped, as indicated above, to his body). Even as the boy is handling the small germ, the large puppet germ is watching; and, of course, later the large germ seizes the paper boy in its mouth.

Whoever insults his brother shall be liable.
—Matthew 5:22

24. The Hammer Head

One day, in the middle of the night, I heard a sound like this [emit two short groans and a long quavery groan]. I got out of bed to see what was going on. The noise was coming from my tool chest. It was my hammer groaning.

"Help! help! help!" screamed my hammer. "I'm dying from a headache." I gave him a bottle of aspirin, and he swallowed the whole bottle. I doubt if it did him much good, because he didn't unscrew the cap before he swallowed it.

When the doctor came my hammer asked him to please fix his head.

"Your head nothing," snorted the doctor. "You've got heart trouble."

The doctor examined his heart and found that it had shrunk so small that it could scarcely be seen. He told the hammer that his headache was caused by the fact that he was always knocking other people, that is, he was always saying bad things about them; and that every time he said something bad about someone, his heart shrank a little more. The doctor also told him that Jesus said that it is wrong for us to be angry with other people or insult them.

"God made us to love each other, instead of hurting each other. No wonder you feel sick," added the doctor.

But do you know what? My hammer did not pay any attention to the doctor, but kept right on knocking people. The more he did it the more his heart shrank and the more his head hurt. It is pretty stupid being a hammer head.

Object Lesson Application

Display a hammer, or a cardboard cutout of one, on which a frown, like that indicated in the picture illustration, has been painted.

72

Picture or Chalk Talk Application

Draw as illustrated. This drawing is made in two stages. The heavy lines indicate the initial stage, which just shows a hammer. The lighter lines show how the hammer is changed into a face. The lighter series of lines is drawn after the heavy ones have been completed. The heavy and light lines are a device for showing the two stages of the drawing and not an indication of relative line thickness to be used in the presentation.

After you have turned your hammer into a face, remark that a lot of people are hammer heads in that they knock others, and of course hurt themselves.

Puppet Talk Application

Use a glove puppet that has been made into a hammer (see pp. 100-101). Have the doctor remove the puppet's heart and show it to the congregation. This is done by having a tiny red paper heart hidden between the thumb and index and middle fingers of your free hand. Reach under the puppet's skirt, and slide the heart forward with your thumb so that it can be seen, and apparently remove this little heart from inside the puppet.

Ask and it will be given you; seek and
you will find.—Matthew 7:7

25. Aladdin's Pocketbook

There was a boy named Wilbur who read a story about a man named Aladdin. Aladdin had a lamp that when rubbed would produce a magician who would do anything Aladdin wanted. How Wilbur wished that he had a lamp like that! He wanted a magician to come and do his homework, mow the lawn, and give him a great big, really truly elephant to go elephant back riding on.

Wilbur remembered reading in his Bible the words, "Ask and it will be given you; seek and you will find." He knelt down by his bed and prayed for a long, long time for a magician. Then he got a jar and rubbed it. To his great surprise he heard a voice.

"Let me out, let me out!" it cried.

But the voice did not come from the jar. It seemed to be coming from his pants pocket. It was coming from his wallet. He took the wallet out of his pocket. The voice was coming from a dollar bill inside the wallet.

"I am a magic dollar," cried the dollar. "I can spread the love of God anywhere in the world. You can use me to feed hungry people, or heal sick people, or make blind people see, or to send people to tell folks all over the world about Jesus, so they can have the wonderful joy of loving him."

"Boy," exclaimed Wilbur, "you are just as good as a magician in a lamp! I wish all dollars were like you."

"All dollars could do wonderful things for God, if people would ony give them a chance to do his work," replied the dollar.

"Could you tell me," asked Wilbur, "is that more important than having a magician to do my homework, mow the lawn, and give me a really truly elephant?"

"I'm sorry," answered the dollar, "that's a question you'll have to decide for yourself."

Object Lesson Application

Display a pocketbook, or a brown construction paper envelope made to look like one. Take a toy money dollar bill out of the pocketbook at the appropriate time. Show that the bill has a picture of Jesus on it (pasted on the bill in advance). Be sure to tell the congregation that it is not Jesus who is in the pocketbook, but that a dedicated dollar can do the work of Jesus.

Picture or Chalk Talk Illustration

Draw as illustrated, drawing the pocketbook first.

Puppet Talk Illustration

Use a hand or glove puppet. Have a paper pocketbook prepared in the manner indicated above, inside the puppet's skirt. Develop the lesson as indicated above. The puppet is cast in the role of Wilbur, and he converses with the sermonizer. (See p. 102.)

The puppet tells the sermonizer that he is trying to duplicate the effects of Aladdin's lamp. The puppet is shown rubbing a small jar. The sermonizer then hears the voice of the dollar bill in the puppet's "pocket." The sermonizer also hears the dollar bill's message. This is done by putting one's ear close to the bill and using the formula, "I can hear the dollar bill saying —————— [complete the dollar's message]." Wilbur then asks the sermonizer the concluding question in the story and the sermonizer gives him the answer given by the dollar in the story.

If any man would come after me, let him
deny himself and take up his cross daily
and follow me.—Luke 9:23

26. The Girl Who Treated Jesus like Junk

A little girl named Inertia had a doll that she dearly loved. She combed its hair, bathed it, and carefully sewed new clothes for it. The more she did for the doll, the more she loved it, for that is the way people are. The more they give of themselves for a cause, the dearer that cause becomes to their hearts. Inertia would not go to sleep at night unless her doll was in bed with her.

However a few years later, Inertia got tired of her doll. Instead of its being her precious baby, it was just junk to her. Its hair was pulled out. Its body was dirty. She never played with it, but left it lying in the dust on her closet floor. She would kick it out of the way when she got dresses out of the closet.

When her mother finally threw the doll away, Inertia just laughed, "I never play with that junky doll anyway."

The sad part of our story is that Inertia treated Jesus the same way she did her doll. Once she loved him very much and went to church school, said her prayers, and listened to her mother read Bible stories. When she got older she stopped doing these things for Jesus, and her faith became just a lot of junk to her, like her old doll, because you never value something when you do not work at it.

Inertia still thought of herself as a Christian, but she would never make any sacrifice for her Savior. When her favorite television program was on, she did not attend church youth meetings.

One day Uncle Mort and his family came to visit for several days. Inertia's cousin Carol was there too. Inertia felt sorry for Carol. She was crippled by polio and could not get out of her wheel chair. However, Carol was always bubbling over with joy. She never thought about herself but was always trying to help someone else. She had a wonderful faith in God. Inertia began to admire her very much. Inertia wished that she had a faith like that of Carol.

Inertia remembered how close Jesus had seemed to her a few years ago. One night she got down on her knees to pray. Suddenly she began to cry.

Her mother came running in to ask, "What on earth is the matter, dear?"

"Oh, Mother," sobbed Inertia, "I tried to pray but I couldn't because Jesus was no longer in my heart. All I had left for a faith was a pile of junk."

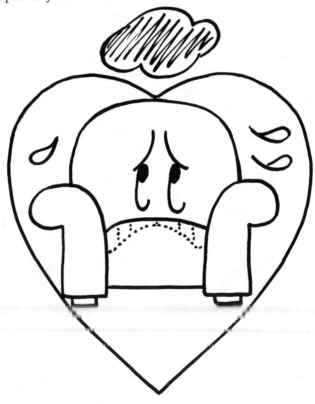

General Lesson Application

See the General Lesson Application for Story 10.

Object Lesson Application

Display an easy chair, drawn from our illustration, or a cutout from a mail order catalogue, or doll furniture; or display a hammock. The hammock is a paper napkin held at diagonally opposite corners and pinched to form a ridge down the center. A picture of a girl from a mail order catalogue is pasted in place as though lying on it. The back side of the napkin may have a frowning face and the word, "Emptiness" painted on it. Remark that Inertia is the kind of a Christian who would rather recline in an easy chair (hammock) than work for Jesus. She is an Easy Chair (Hammock) Christian. At the proper time in the story, turn the chair (hammock) around and show the word "Emptiness" written on the back. The faith of the lazy Christian is empty and unrewarding. Of course salvation is not gained through works, but one's love for God must be strong enough to motivate works, if it is a true love.

Picture or Chalk Talk Application

Draw first the heart; then the easy chair within it. Using the lesson application given above, indicate that Inertia is an Easy Chair Christian. Her love for God is an "easy chair love." The heart represents her love for God, and the chair within identifies it as lazy. The dissatisfaction brought on by a lazy faith is shown by the sad facial features on the chair, the cloud of gloom overhead, and the drops of "anxiety" emanating from the heart. These features are added to the drawing only at the end of the story. The dotted lines on our sample drawing should be drawn with continuous lines as a part of the sad expression. They are drawn here with dotted lines to differentiate them from the line that represents the seat of the chair, and which line serves the dual purpose of being also a part of the frown. This "seat line" is drawn initially with the drawing of the chair.

Puppet Talk Application

Use a hand or glove puppet. Use the presentation given in the object lesson application with the following modifications: The puppet is described as being a "lazy Christian." This laziness is symbolized by showing the puppet asleep on a hymnbook, with a handkerchief used as a blanket over it. The puppet is unhappy as a result of this spiritual sloth. At the proper time in the story, the puppet's heart is taken out of its costume and shown. It is a red paper heart and it has the word "Emptiness" written on it.

CHILDREN'S
SERMON TECHNIQUES

STORY SERMONS

Criteria of Suitability

Children's sermons should be adapted to the understanding of a child. For instance, a sermon on humility might better deal with children who show off in front of their class, instead of telling how a general in the army was humble enough to help some private dig a ditch. A sermon on the nature of God might better compare his love to that of an earthly parent, than to deal with the nature of the Trinity. A small child does not have enough understanding of the nature of the members of the Trinity individually, to make even the simplest explanation of the Trinity of meaning to him.

Another example of a poor children's sermon is one where the teacher holds up a clear pane of glass and a mirror, declaring that the love of money is evil because the silvered mirror back, in contrast with the clear glass, prevents one from seeing other people through it, but rather limits one's gaze to himself. Whereas a child is old enough to share his allowance in the work of Christ, he is not old enough to be in a position where monetary considerations could dominate his life and shut out his sensitivity to others.

In preparing a children's sermon, one should ask himself whether or not he has ever seen, or heard of, a child actually doing the things about which he would speak. If, after a children's sermon, a parent is able to say to a child, "See, the minister was talking about you this morning," it is an indication that the talk was appropriate.

Although children's sermons should usually be about things that children actually do, this should not rule out the inclusion of stories about the lives of great people. A child is quite capable of having such stories mold his life. Whereas a child cannot immediately do such a thing as serve as a foreign missionary, he can think about such things. A child's goals and concepts of his future self are very much a part of his present life.

One should be careful not to talk down to a child. A child's understanding is far more advanced than his ability to express himself. A small child can draw a picture of a man that consists of stick-like arms and legs coming off a big, round, bodyless head. However the same child would immediately know that something was wrong if he saw a lifelike doll that had the body omitted. Children watch television and are observers of the adult world, and understand more of this world than many people realize.

One should avoid the story-sermon that uses a moral of vague relationship to the story. If a story is to be about a childish foible, let it be about that foible from start to finish. For example, one should avoid telling a story about how an aviator flew his plane high enough to make a rat in it die of oxygen starvation, and then urging children to similarly live on a high plane. Flying an airplane high is not the same as living on a high level. Furthermore, although one can avoid certain temptations through a highly moral life, and although heights do kill rats, it is not true that moral living avoids temptations *because* heights kill rats.

Methods of Gaining Interest

To add interest and better to strike home with a moral, a children's sermon should be specific in identifying faults or virtues. Do not merely say, "Sonny is a gossip," but say, "Sonny said, 'Joe has a big, fat mother.'" Do not say, "Sonny gave money to benevolences," but say, "Sonny gave his fifty cents to help a little boy in India learn to love Jesus." Do not say, "The children were always fighting," but say, "Sally ran to Mother yelling, 'Mommy, Sonny is spitting on me!'"

It will be helpful, in preparing children's sermons, to keep a record of the actual good and bad deeds of children that one knows.

A story will hold juvenile interest far better than a lecture that consists of only one moralizing sentence after another. If one is sensitive to audience empathy, it is possible to sense interest rapidly waning at the point where one completes a children's story-sermon and starts tacking a moral onto it.

Regardless of whether a children's sermon is an object sermon or not, it is advantageous for it to be centered around a mental picture of an object that is captivating to the imagination. It is easier for a child to remember stories about such themes as dirty pigs that gossip, or irreverent donkeys in church, or selfish octopuses, than it is for him to remember such abstract themes as "kindness in speech," or "reverence in church,' or "sharing one's possessions."

If an actual object or picture is shown with a sermon, retention is increased many fold. Three days after Sunday, many a child would be able to say, "I saw a pig in church that said bad things"; but how many would be able even to remember the theme of an abstract sermon on kindliness in speech?

Much of the success of a children's sermon depends upon the skill of the speaker. The sermon should be practiced in advance, until all the details come readily to mind without notes. The sermon is more likely to be effective if the speaker enjoys himself in giving it. It is also helpful if he is a good actor, so that he can portray the emotions of his characters with his voice, and illustrate their actions with his gestures. When a story character speaks, it should not sound as though the narrator were speaking for him, but as though the character himself were speaking. The speaker should learn to sense the reactions of his congregation, so that he can know if their interest is being held, and if they are experiencing the desired emotions.

Depth of Content

The children's sermon should be simple without being shallow. Many of the great doctrines of the church can be taught through them. At the heart of the teaching program there should be the belief that every child needs to grow toward finding fullness of life through complete commitment to the Savior. For instance, the teaching should go beyond merely urging Junior to share his toys just for the sake of sharing. He should know that the real reason for sharing is because he belongs to Christ, and that this is Christ's way for him to live. Whereas such concepts as the life in Christ being a better one of peace and joy, now and forever, and the life without him being one of frustration, emptiness, and sadness, and the loss of eternal life, should not be preached to a child in adult terms, they can still be taught implicitly within the story-sermon.[1]

1 Story-sermons 3, 4, 7, 10, (among others) cite the joy of living for Christ. Story-sermon 22 tells of the promise of eternal life for Christians. Story-sermons 1, 6, 8, 12, 14, 26 (among others) cite the problems that come from the neglect of Christ.

When to Use Story-Sermons

Story-sermons, with visual aids to add interest, can be used almost any time children are gathered together for worship or religious instruction. In addition to the usual times on Sunday morning, they can be used in vacation Bible schools or junior youth fellowship services. For instance, story-sermon 22 is concerned with a basic problem of youth — the desire for popularity and the need for the self-esteem gained from recognition from others, and could be used as part of a youth program. In addition to the use of this story, material could be presented from real life, showing how some people are gloriously happy through expending themselves for others, and how others are miserable because they worry about what people think of them. Discussion questions could be asked about why young people showoff, why people need recognition from others, and how and why faith provides the answers to this problem.

Story-sermons 2, 9, 15, 18, 20, 24, and 25 are all taken from the Sermon on the Mount, and could be used as supplementary material in a study of this topic.

OBJECT LESSONS

How to Add Teaching Material to the Story-Sermons in This Book, in Adapting Them to Their Visual Applications.

A story can sometimes be made more forceful if a sermon is included in it as a part of the story. For instance, in story-sermon 11, one of Willie's hairs quotes Scripture and preaches to him. However, the sermon is only three sentences long and is a basic part of the plot. Willie must hear the hair's message if he is to reform.

Any story can have more teaching material added to it through the above method. If the story does not have a character in it to give a lecture (which will include the added teaching material) to the hero, such a character can be added. Many of the stories in this book will need the use of this method in adapting the story to the visual presentations. For instance, story-sermon 3, in its object lesson presentation, features a device for cripples to wear or use. In introducing this device, one could have Junior's father, in explaining what the Wobble, Wobble, Flops were, show Junior a crutch and say that nobody wants to have to use crutches because they are a sign of weak, helpless legs, and similarly the lack of practice will make a person weak and helpless in the area where he has failed to work.

How to Convert Any Children's Sermon into an Object Lesson Sermon

With a little thought it is possible to convert any children's sermon into an object lesson sermon. If the sermon is a story-sermon, it will be about an object, an animal, or a person. In the former cases, merely show the object or animal in actual, miniature, or pictorial form. If the story is about people, it will still have an abstract theme, such as "love," "greed," or "vanity," which can be pictured in a symbolic way. Thus a heart, a pig, and a peacock could symbolize these themes respectively. A children's story-sermon can be revised for the introduction of a symbolic object, by substituting a humanized object or animal to act the part of a person in the story; or by

87

allowing the object to come in contact with that person. For instance, a cloud of gloom could settle over a person's head, or a frown could be shown on his heart, or his head could change into that of a mule, or he could observe an animal or an object and learn from it. The story-sermons in this book are examples of these methods.

If a children's sermon is not in story form, one could display a symbolic object to represent the sermon theme, after altering the sermon to let this object play a prominent part in the sermon.

With enough thought, any children's sermon can be adapted into an object sermon. After thinking of a symbolic object adaptation for a sermon, it is often advisable to think further, and come up with something simpler or more appropriate than the initial idea.

How to Convert Object Lessons into Story Form

Object sermons can usually be improved by telling them in story form. To do this, think up some trouble or blessing that could logically (or illogically, if you want to let your imagination run wild) happen to that type of person, animal, or object, from success or failure in observing the sermon moral. If trouble results, the re-formation of the character and a happy ending is optional.

Suitability of Objects

Discretion should be shown in the selection of objects for use in children's sermons. The object should emphasize the point of the story, rather than calling attention to itself. For instance, the first story in this book teaches the idea that selfishness brings unhappiness. The use of a grabby octopus enforces this concept. However if a person put a toy octopus in a bag, and then made a toy truck disappear and reappear in the bag with the octopus, the wrong things would be emphasized. The children would be more apt to remember the fact that a truck had magically disappeared, or that a octopus had a magic affinity for a truck, than to remember the lesson on selfishness. The flashy technique would call attention to itself, rather than being a servant of the moral. Magic and chemical object lessons can be of value, but the great danger in their use is that they so often appear to be showy effects with morals hitched to them as an afterthought.

A teaching object should be as simple as possible, as a rule. Complicated object lessons can be distracting.

A teaching object should represent an idea with a natural or a generally accepted relationship. For instance, the use of a pig to represent a dirty person is natural, because when one thinks of a pig he automatically thinks of a filthy sty. A glass of water that changes color chemically from clear to black would be a weaker such representation, because the congregation would never think of it as standing for dirt, unless the speaker so labeled it.

The Construction of Teaching Objects

Two-dimensional objects, or objects made of paper that folds or bends to take on a three-dimensional form, are preferable to solid objects because they are much easier to store. It is easier to use colored construction paper than it is to use paints in achieving colors. Colored paper also comes in gummed form. Felt pointed marking pens are the fastest way of outlining a paper surface. Latex house paint is a handy way to paint a large surface, as it dries rapidly and the brushes can be cleaned with water.

It is advisable to make objects as quickly and simple as possible. People in religious work usually have many demands on their time, so the making of intricate objects is not worth the investment in time. Simple objects are just as effective as elaborate ones. Simple rectangular and oval shapes can be put together to represent any object or animal. If their shape is not true enough to life to identify them, they can be labeled orally as they are introduced. A green oval or triangle on top of a thin, brown rectangle will do just as well to represent a tree as an intricately detailed model. An elephant can be made out of an oval, a half oval, and three rectangles. This principle is well illustrated by the drawings of two trees, an elephant, a giraffe, a pig, a dog, and a kangaroo. The geometric shapes can be held together with paper clips or brass paper fasteners. If holes are punched for the latter, motion can be given to animal legs.

One advantage in the use of simple geometric forms is that a lot of bright colors can be used, where they would not look right in a more lifelike representation. For instance, an elephant could be shown with a green leg, a red leg, a white body, a blue head, and an orange trunk. The bright colors would appeal to children.

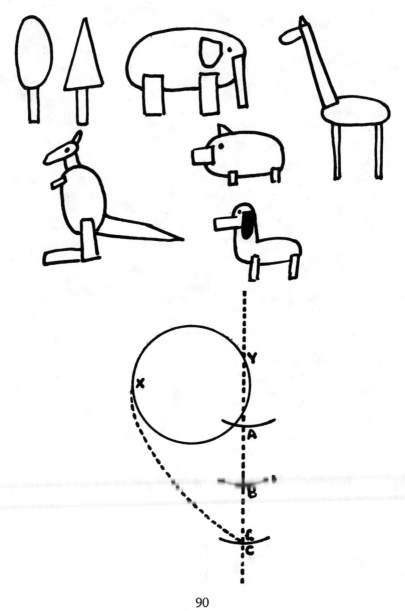

Because of the frequent use this book makes of hearts in illustrating object lessons, a simple formula is given for their construction. In following these instructions refer to the drawing of the circle. Draw a line so that it barely passes through a circle. (The dotted straight line in the drawing). Mark off three lengths of the radius of the circle from one point where the line crosses the circle. (A, B, and C are the arcs, drawn with a compass, that indicate the length of three radii from the point of intersection at Y.) Fold the paper along the straight line and mark off a curving line between the third radius and the part of the circle farthest from the straight line (from C to X). Cut along this curved line, cutting through both thicknesses of the folded paper, and follow the line of the circle, when you come to it, around to the point of juncture with the crease in the paper. (Cut along the curved line from C to Y.)

A simpler method is to fold a paper and make the above cut by guess, without making markings. A satisfactory symmetrical heart should result.

Sources of Animal Sermon Ideas

Ideas for animal sermons can be gotten from nature books, Aesop's *Fables,* and the Bible. See also: Jacob J. Sessler, *Story Talks from Animal Life,* Fleming H. Revell Company, Westwood, New Jersey, 1956.

PICTURE AND CHALK TALKS

Picture Talks

Many readers will not feel able to give chalk talks, but it is worth a try. Those who cannot master this art may draw the pictures in advance, with a felt point pen, on stiff 18″ by 24″ paper. Or they may get an artist friend to draw them. They will then be able to hold up the completed pictures during talks. In instances where chalk talk pictures are to be drawn in two stages of development, two completed drawings could be shown.

Chalk Talk Materials

CHALK — Lecturers chalk crayons are 3″ long, and either ½″ or 1″ square. The larger size is for shading with colors, while the smaller size is usually used for black outlining.

PAPER — 24″ x 36″ newsprint is the standard size. Some people prefer 36″ x 48″ paper, or this size cut down to 36″ x 40″. Many sheets of paper are used on a drawing board to provide a padded surface for drawing.

BALL BEARING CLIPS — Hold paper to easel. Clips that are 1⅜″ wide can be used for drawing boards ¼″ thick. Clips that are 2½″ wide will be needed for ½″ thick boards.

WHERE TO OBTAIN — These items may be obtained through an art or stationery store, or school art department. If necessary, a newspaper may help you find a source for a large size of newsprint.

EASELS — A simple easel can be made by placing a drawing board on top of a table and leaning the board against a wall. Rubber matting at the top and bottom of the board would protect table and wall surfaces. The easel can also lean against the flat back of a chair, placed on top of the table. Rubber matting under the chair will protect the table, and heavy books placed on it will keep it from slipping. A sturdy card table can be used for the table.

A piece of plastic or newspaper may be used to protect carpeting from falling chalk.

The drawing board should be the same width as the paper and

either the same height or 4" to 6" higher, for added height in drawing. The paper would be clipped to the top and bottom of the board. The backs of the corners of the board could be chiseled down to ¼" in width if you wish to use 1⅜" clips.

Here are instructions for making a simple table-top easel. A sturdy card table provides the portable bottom section. See the diagram.

Cut a piece of ½" x 2' x 3' plywood diagonally into two triangles (labeled "X" in the diagram). Take one of the triangles and measure 3" along the hypotenuse, from the angle made by the junction of the hypotenuse with the 2' side, and mark this point ("A" in the diagram). Draw a line between point A and the right angle of the triangle (point "B"). Cut along this line. (The dotted lines at the bottom of the triangles in the diagram indicate the wood that has been cut off.) Do this with the other triangle. These triangles are the sides of the easel.

A second ½" x 2' x 3' piece of plywood will become the drawing board. (This piece labeled "Y" in the diagram.) Fasten a ½" by 3"

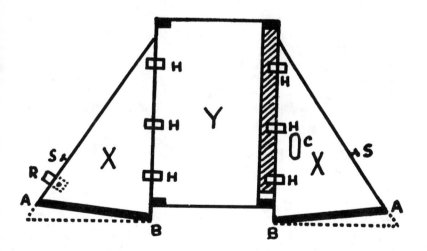

strip of plywood to one side of the drawing board with glue and screws. This will come down to within 3" of the bottom of the board, and will allow the sides of the easel to stack in together when it is folded. (This strip is shown with diagonal shading lines on it in the diagram.)

Secure the sides to the drawing board with hinges, placing them as indicated. (Labeled "H" in the diagram.) Place the sides so they extend 3" below the bottom of the easel.

Rubber matting should be stapled around the bottom of the easel sides to protect tables and give traction. (This matting is shown in black in the diagram.)

The black areas at the corners of the drawing board represent the areas that are chiseled from the back side, so that they can hold 1⅜" ball bearing clips.

With the sides folded in, hold the easel so that its length extends out horizontally, and find the balance point. Make a "hand hole" in the side that folds outermost. (The long narrow oval, labeled "C" in the diagram represents a hand hole.) This will serve as a carrying handle.

A simple catch will hold the easel sides folded in. A thin strip of wood, 1½" x 2½", with a screw in its center, and fastened near the bottom of the side that folds innermost, will turn to lap over the outermost side. This strip is labeled "R" in the diagram. (The dotted lines show that part of it which lies behind the side.) The dot represents the screw.

LIGHTS — If lighting is needed for your easel, a desk lamp will do. It should have a flexible arm and a bullet-shaped metal shade to focus the light. The best place for it is on the floor in front of your easel. You can also use an adjustable clamp-on lamp fastened to the top of the easel. The lamp should be connected to an extension cord with a switch on it, so that the switch can be on the table where it is handy for you.

If an overhead lamp is used, it will be necessary to anchor the sides to keep the easel from tipping over frontwards. Fasten some screws to the easel sides near the bottom. (These screws are labeled "S" in the diagram.) Loop springs over these screws and fasten hooks into the loops in the other ends of the springs. These hooks can be made of thick wire obtained by cutting up a coat hanger. The hooks will hook under the bottom of the card table in the back. These devices can be easily slipped on and off.

BLACKBOARD — Paper can be saved by practicing drawings on a blackboard. Masonite painted with blackboard paint is the cheapest source of a blackboard.

Chalk Drawing

Anyone can use simple chalk drawings with children's sermons, no matter how poorly he draws. The important thing is to illustrate a point, not to show off drawing skill. If the speaker makes no pretense at being an artist, the crudest of drawings will still be effective. There is something fascinating about even a straight black line being drawn on a big sheet of white paper. Figures 9, 14, and 2 on this page are examples of extremely crude drawings illustrating story-sermons 9, 14, and 2. This level of artistic achievement could be achieved by any third grader, yet it is still effective.

If a picture is outlined lightly in advance with blue pencil, these lines will be invisible to a congregation.

Always stand to one side as you draw, so your audience can watch the picture progress. The key lines in a picture of a person are the lines of the mouth and eyes in the face. These should be drawn last, with the eyes usually drawn after the mouth, to give a climactic

finish. When shading in an area, thick, three-inch wide strokes should be made with the side of the chalk, splashing strokes sketchily over the area, rather than filling it in solid, as this adds speed to your drawing.

Talcum powder, applied in advance to the hands, will make them easier to clean. A dark-colored, moist cloth, kept on the table behind the easel, can be used to wipe most of the chalk off the hands, after the talk.

A helpful book is: Bert J. Griswold, *Crayon and Character*, Meigs Publishing Company, Indianapolis, Indiana, 1913.

Chalk Talk Supplies can be secured from Balda Art Service, Oshkosh, Wisconsin.

PUPPETRY

Two-Faced Hand Puppets

By adding an extra face to the back of a puppet's head and operating the puppet with both sides of the hand toward the audience, one can have a single puppet represent two people, or show two expressions. By painting one face a symbolic color, one can use this color as a teaching aid. Thus you could represent your puppet as being red in anger, or green with envy or illness. Also blue would show gloom, yellow would show cowardice or Midas-like love of gold, green would show growth, and purple would show royalty, or our sonship with God.

One may make a two-faced puppet by taping a cylinder of paper around the head of any hand puppet, such as are carried in the Christmas catalogues of large mail order companies or are in the catalogues of some non-denominational Sunday school supply publishing companies. One should paint large features on both sides of the paper. A smile on one side and a frown on the other will be useful for showing changes in emotion.

Light Bulb Hand Puppets

A light bulb puppet is made by removing the head from a standard hand puppet and sticking the bottom of a sixty-watt light bulb through the neck of the costume. The bulb is screwed into a light socket, on an extension cord, which is inside the costume. The thumb and index finger work the arms, while the lower three fingers clasp the socket and work the push-in type switch. Two white 4"x6" filing cards, glued into a 8¼" long strip are formed into a cylinder around the light bulb and held with paper clips. The top of the cylinder is narrower than the bottom to hold it on the bulb. A face is painted on the outside of the cylinder and additional features are painted on the inside, so that the expression of the face will change when the light is on.

The face can also change color, when the light is on, if a cylinder of typing paper, which has been colored with a felt point marking pen, is inserted inside the face cylinder. Instead of coloring this inner liner solidly, one might paint a cross or other symbol on it. However, this cross should shine through simpler facial features than those on the face cylinders described below.

This page shows a diagram of a face that changes from sadness (painted on the outside of the cylinder) to joy (painted on the inside) when the light bulb is turned on. the outside of the cylinder is painted a light flesh color, except the oval eye whites are left white. The shaded areas, in the bottom of the whites, are colored

with a mixture of flesh and red, and are on the *inside* of the face cylinder. Dotted lines around the eyes represent heavy black lines on the inside of the cylinder. On the outside of the cylinder, the eyebrows are black, the irises blue, the pupils black with white highlights, the lines almost around the eyes are black, the nose is red with a black line around the bottom, and the frowning mouth (shown drawn with solid lines) is light red and *not* outlined with black. The lips on the inside of the cylinder (outlined with dotted lines) are bright red, the shaded mouth area is painted with a thick layer of black, and the teeth are white outlined with black.

The face that changes from a smile to a frown, diagramed on this page, is made along the same lines as the above one, with broken lines and shaded areas showing inside coloration and solid lines.

showing outside coloration; and the same colors are used in comparable places, except the eyebrows are on the inside instead of the outside, black lines are added under the corners of the mouth on the inside, and there are no flesh-colored areas under the eyes on the inside of the cylinder.

The puppet costume should have cloth hands (so that your extended fingers push against the extremities of the hands), if you wish to lengthen the arms. The arms are lengthened by sewing longer cloth arms over the original ones, which are left the same length. The lengthened area is stuffed with cotton. The longer arms allow the puppet to reach two or more inches higher along its head.

A Glove Puppet

A glove puppet can be made from a very large, tan, cotton sock. See below for a diagram. Cut a slit (A) in the toe of the sock and sew a piece of red corduroy, reinforced with felt or interlon, around the cut edges of the sock so that a red mouth is formed (fig. 2). Large, round, cardboard eyes have brown irises, black pupils, white highlights, are rimmed with heavy black lines, and are glued to the sock. A pink cloth or felt tongue may be added. Stitches, on either side of where the thumb comes in the lower jaw, connecting the bottom of the jaw with the red lower mouth, will give better control of the mouth action.

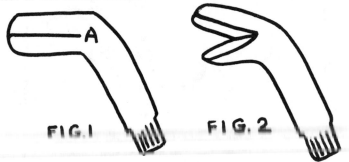

This glove puppet can be made into a dog by pinning on a black paper nose and long, hang-down ears. Put the ears on pointing upwards and it is a donkey. Make the ears short and pointed and add a body made of part of a sock with black spots on it, and it is a leopard. Add an oval pink nose with black nostrils and put the hand in the puppet upside down, with the thumb in the upper mouth and the four fingers in the jaw, and it is a pig. Remove nose and ears, and it is a worm. A bird is made by merely pinning paper wings to either side of the sock body. A skunk is made by sticking the regular head into a body made from a black sock. Part of the sock extends out as a tail. A white strip of cloth is sewn down the back of the body and tail. No legs are needed Shorten a paper bag and work the puppet inside the bag through a hole in the bottom and it is an oyster in its shell. Pin eight paper arms to the puppet body and it is an octopus. By sewing the toe of a sock in the shape of a trunk and pinning this over the upper mouth, you can make an elephant. Pin on appropriate paper tails, legs, ears, and it can form any number of animals.

The glove puppet can be made into a candle by placing a paper orange flame in its mouth and by pinning on a two-dimensional picture of a candle holder to its base. The candle is first shown to the audience with the lower jaw toward them, so that the eyes are out of sight. It can be made into a hammer by clenching the hand inside the puppet into a fist, and pinning on a two-dimensional picture of a hammer head to the head of the puppet. One's free hand should clasp the bottom of the puppet sleeve as though one were holding a hammer. The first is unclenched when the puppet moves its mouth. A cactus is made by pinning a paper "L" shaped and spinose cactus limb to the puppet under the lower jaw.

Puppet Manipulation

One can hold a conversation with a puppet by having it respond to questions by shaking its head "yes" or "no," or by having it whisper in your ear, while you repeat what it "says," as though making sure you heard what it said correctly. The puppet should be interesting to watch, by being full of short, lively motions.